Beginning E⬚
with young children

by Opal Dunn

Essential Language Teaching Series

General Editor: Monica Vincent and Roger H Flavell

MODERN ENGLISH PUBLICATIONS

First published 1983
Reprinted 1985, 1989, 1990, 1991

Published by MACMILLAN PUBLISHERS LTD
London and Basingstoke

ISBN 0-333-33307-1

The author and publishers are grateful to
Longman Group Ltd for permission
to reproduce an illustration
from *Dippitydoo: Songs and
Activities for Children* by Sheila
Aristotelous Ward.

Contents

About this book

This book is the result of many years of teaching and training teachers of young children in the Far East, Europe and North Africa. It is written for teachers of young children. In this context young children cannot be thought of only in chronological terms; personal development and cultural background play an important role in the readiness of a child to learn. Bearing this in mind, the book is written for teachers of children from pre-school age up to as late as ten or eleven years. The emphasis is on the earlier years.

In this book, the terms *EFL*, *ESL* and *bilingual* are used to describe the learning situations found in schools and classrooms throughout the world. Figure 3 gives examples of where the terms can be applied. Language 1 is taken to refer to the mother tongue, or the language used in school if it is other than the mother tongue. For convenience, English is mostly referred to as Language 2 (L2). The child is referred to as 'he' and the teacher as 'she', as most of the teachers the author has met are women.

Examples that make abstract ideas concrete are taken from the author's experience. These, together with charts, checklists and other illustrative material, should make the book helpful to teachers in EFL, ESL or bilingual teaching situations.

Many people believe that children in EFL, ESL or bilingual learning situations all pass through approximately the same beginning stages, acquiring language in more or less the same order. For convenience, the author refers to these stages as Part One of a syllabus. Chapter 2 looks at this in more detail. By the end of Part One, children can use a little language well and are ready, in Part Two, to cope with the wider syllabus and more varied and less predictable activities of a language-learning programme. This book is principally concerned with Part One of a beginner's syllabus. The final chapter of *Developing English with young learners* (Dunn 1984: Chapter 5) focuses on Part Two of such a syllabus.

The language young beginners learn to read and write must already be within their oral vocabulary. For this reason, this book deals with oral acquisition and *Developing English with young learners* develops reading, handwriting and writing skills. *Beginning English with young children* introduces young children's language learning strategies which cannot be divorced from their developmental needs. Ideas are given on how to adapt an existing syllabus and plan a programme. Details on how to begin oral communication and suggestions for games, rhymes and songs complete the book.

Local situations differ from country to country and classroom to classroom, and each child is an individual requiring individual attention. For this reason, there can obviously be no one teaching method and no one text suitable for all children. What is written in this book is based on experience and study and an effort to see things not only from the teacher's point of view, but also from the child's. The intention and hope is that it should be flexible enough to be used in the wide variety of situations throughout the world in which English is taught to young beginners.

1 Young children and language learning

'We become interested in what we are good at', to quote Bruner (in Donaldson 1978: 124). This simple truth about attitudes also applies to learning English. How often adults say, 'I like English. I was good at it', or conversely when excusing their poor English add, 'I was never any good at it at school'.

Young children, if they are normal, want to learn. 'At no other time in life does the human being display such enthusiasm for learning, for living, for finding out' (Pluckrose 1979: 27). Life-long attitudes appear to be formed early. If teachers can manage to capture children's enthusiasm and keep it by presenting well-planned lessons, right for their needs and development level, the children they teach should make progress and find that they are good at English. It is at this first stage of learning English that foundations for what may be a life-long interest in English language and culture can be laid.

1.1 Children's expectations

Children come to English lessons with expectations about what they are going to do and achieve. These expectations are influenced by what the family, friends and society in general expect and what they have heard from other children.

'Children are creatures of the moment. They work best and most successfully when the objectives are clear, comprehensible, immediate' (Pluckrose 1979: 27). Children want to please; they care about what others think about them. They want immediate results. They expect to go home after the first lesson able to speak some English, so that they can be praised by their parents and show off to their friends. They long to be able to talk a lot of English quickly, in a grown-up manner. Children are used to communicating in Language 1 and as soon as possible they want to do the same in English. They expect to use English in real experiences. They want to be able to talk about things that interest them, that are vital to them. Only as they grow older are they interested in things outside their immediate surroundings.

If they are already reading and writing in Language 1, they expect to be taught to do the same in English. Although pre-school children are happy with the same all-oral approach they have in Language 1, to spend months only speaking English is not 'real school work' to children who can read and write. *Developing English with young learners* (Dunn 1984) explains how reading and writing can be brought into the children's planned programme of learning.

If children do not get what they have expected in the English lesson, they are disappointed. If parents do not get what they have expected and cannot see progress, they are disappointed too. Parents' enthusiasm can motivate; their disappointment can reflect on their children, causing them to lose interest.

1.2 Starting to learn another language

The debate as to how young children learn another language continues, and is likely to continue, as the number of young children learning English increases and more research becomes available.

The acquisition/learning distinction is not new. It suggests that adults have two independent but interrelated systems for gaining ability in another language: acquisition and learning. The view of

Krashen is that 'The good language learner is an acquirer; he may or may not be a conscious learner' (Krashen 1981: 37). Young children are acquirers. Acquisition takes place subconsciously in situations where speakers communicate naturally. In these situations, speakers are more concerned with the use of language to convey meaning than with correct usage. They want to say something, and without thinking to communicate with the language they know ('use') rather than analyse it in order to find out the correct 'usage' or way to use it. Teaching the rules of usage is not necessary for acquirers.

The other system, 'learning', takes place consciously. 'It is helped greatly by error correction and the presentation of explicit rules' (Krashen and Seliger 1975, quoted in Krashen 1981: 2). In short, it appears that fluency comes unconsciously from what a learner has acquired in interpersonal communication, whilst the formal knowledge of rules has to be learned consciously.

Many young children are still acquiring Language 1. In their desire to communicate (if the circumstances permit), they create situations in which language can be acquired. They are willing to use language and to experiment with sounds, without worrying about mistakes. They rarely have the inhibitions typical of adolescents and adults. When a young child learns another language, he approaches it in the same way as when he learns Language 1: 'his awareness of what he talks about normally takes precedence over his awareness of what he talks with – the words that he uses' (Donaldson 1978: 88). Thus for the maximum language acquisition in the classroom, young children need to be exposed to a programme rich in meaningful, real-life activities in which communication takes place naturally.

Recent research suggests that Language 1 acquisition can be identified on one hand as Gestalt and on the other as analytic or creative. Gestalt psychology stresses the importance of learning by wholes. Gestalt language consists of prefabricated routines or patterns which are memorised as whole utterances (see Figure 1).

Figure 1

Analytic or creative language	Gestalt or prefabricated language

Creative language Includes labelling and identifying objects. Word by word development, eg
 a dog   a cat
 a brown dog a brown cat
 a dog and cat
	Prefabricated language
	 1 Prefabricated routines
	     Phrases, sentences more complex than a child's linguistic level eg How are you? What are you doing? Rhymes Memorised by imitation
	 2 Prefabricated patterns
	     Phrases, sentences part memorised part creative language. Creative language changeable, prefabricated language constant

Language input	
Regular Consciously graded, clear, easy-to-imitate (but not unnatural) speech ('caretaker speech' – see page 51)	Very frequent repetition Quick 'conversational type' prefabricated language used socially, in games and classroom organisation (see Chapter 3) Simple patterns eg This is . . .
Use	
In beginning lessons, less used and developed than prefabricated. Gradual input and memorisation until balance between creative and prefabricated nearly equal at end Part I. Part II language acquisition situations less predictable, creative language becomes dominant	From first lesson very frequent repetition. Short cut to allow immediate communication with minimum linguistic competence. Due to Language 1 experience, child more able to imitate and memorise and relies on this ability. As creative language develops, less used in activities except for socialising and organising

By contrast, analytic or creative language develops word by word and utterances are consciously constructed by the speaker. In the initial stages of learning, prefabricated language is more used; however, all learners develop use of creative language which eventually dominates. Research indicates that for many Language 2 learners, especially children, Gestalt speech (prefabricated language) serves as a short cut to allow social interaction and interpersonal communication with a minimum of linguistic competence. The analytic or creative mode begins to predominate as learners attempt to express specific and possibly individual ideas.

The linguistic environment of the classroom is conducive to learning prefabricated patterns and routines. A programme which follows the same framework, with familiar and new activities slotted into it, gives children an opportunity to predict the meaning of the language used, since much of it, for example the organisation language, will be the same. With regular repetition of the same prefabricated language, children quickly understand situations and memorise the language involved. It appears that children learning another language have a great capacity to imitate and memorise long utterances as they have already had to do this when learning Language 1. Once a child has memorised some prefabricated language, he has a feeling he can speak 'a lot of English' and as soon as he has understood how to transfer language (see also Chapter 4), he seems to have an ability to use the little language he knows in different situations for maximum communication. When he can communicate with others, he can acquire more language and gradually develop more fluency. Where children are not exposed to planned opportunities to acquire prefabricated language, acquisition is slower. Reliance on prefabricated language is only possible in the predictable situation of a classroom; it is a very helpful tool in fulfilling the children's expectations (referred to in the previous section of this Chapter).

Figure 2 Second-year pupils acting 'The Gingerbread Boy' (Dunn 1979)

Skills learned in one language are not only applicable to that language. Teachers will have noticed when teaching children to count in English that children who already know how to use numbers in Language 1 learn very quickly in English. In fact, they are transferring their concepts of number from Language 1 and merely learning a new linguistic label in English. The same applies to literacy skills. Children who can already read in Language 1, once introduced to reading in English, learn quite quickly. This is partly due to the fact that they are more mature, but also because they already have the literacy skill of reading which they transfer.

Some teachers trying to teach new concepts in English to children who have not already learned them in Language 1 are often left in doubt as to whether the children have really understood. Swain points out that 'instruction in the first language can benefit second language' (1981: 6). Where children have not sufficient oral ability in Language 2, it is a good idea for teachers to wait to teach a new concept in Language 2 until it has been taught in Language 1. Once it has been taught in Language 1, it may be quickly transferred to Language 2.

Some teachers feel that to continue explaining in Language 1 will retard language development in English. Providing the explanation is not given as direct translation or in a way that interferes with language acquisition experiences in Language 2, 'spending time learning in one language benefits both languages equally with respect to developing those language-related skills essential to academic success' (Swain 1981: 5).

CHILD/ADULT LANGUAGE-LEARNING DIFFERENCES

It is thought that an important relationship may exist between physical maturation (puberty) and language acquisition in the early years. Teachers and parents remark how quickly young children acquire another language and how error-free their speech and in particular their pronunciation is, in spite of being given little or no formal grammar instruction. They marvel at young children's ability to imitate, often so well that they are indistinguishable from native speakers. Adults normally retain an accent long after they have reached fluency, whereas children who acquire a second language before puberty usually manage to speak without an accent. A typical example is the adult immigrant who speaks Language 2 with a marked accent whilst his son speaks a neighbourhood dialect indistinguishable from his local friends.

There seems to be no question that puberty is an important turning point in language acquisition. This generally occurs about the age of twelve years. At this time adolescents become capable of thinking abstractly. This may have the effect of increasing their ability to learn language by conscious analysis, but it weakens their acquisition ability. In the words of de Villiers and de Villiers, 'after puberty, language learning seems to proceed more laboriously and is never complete' (de Villiers and de Villiers 1979: 124).

However, linguistic considerations alone are not sufficient in considering how young children learn another language. Young children are still learning concepts and developing skills which affect their ability to acquire language. For this reason, Language 2 cannot be taught as an isolated subject; it has to be thought of in terms of the whole child and his individual educational needs and interests.

1.3 The developing child

Activities which impose what the teacher would wish to take place, but which are beyond the child's level of development, are difficult and even in some cases impossible for the child to understand. They often result in a restless classroom, or discipline problems in large classes.

Without a knowledge of a child's various stages of cognitive, emotional, physical, social and language development, and an ability to recognise these changes, it is difficult for a teacher to plan an effective programme. Piaget's view that all children pass through the same stages of cognitive development but at different rates, still provides a comprehensive outline for the study of intellectual development.

Experienced teachers of young beginners are conscious of these different stages and know how to recognise developmental changes as they take place. Changes can take place within a week or even within a lesson, which means that teachers need to be flexible, adjusting lesson plans where necessary to cope with new developments. In some cases there seem to be periods of concentrated and sometimes rapid development followed by periods of little advance. The inset below gives an actual illustration of this.

AGE	5.3
GROUP SIZE	One
BACKGROUND	Language 1 = English
	Parents both English
SCHOOL	English language primary school in West Malaysia
LEVEL	Beginner Non-reader

One morning during a short school holiday, this little girl brought a pencil and paper to her mother and asked her to show her how to write. Previously she had not been interested in writing. For the next three days she continuously asked for more information and practised writing. On the fourth day she discovered that she could copy the print from her picture books. After copying from some of her books at random, she suddenly stopped writing and changed her activities completely. When she went back to school, she showed her new skill to the teacher and was moved into the special 'writing group' for the few children in the class who could write.

The rate of development may not necessarily indicate a young child's ability. An intelligent child may be a slow developer or even a late developer. Children who make little progress may have some physical difficulty which may not have been recognised (see page 14).

The length of time a child can concentrate on doing one activity also varies from child to child. Some young children can only manage to concentrate for about five minutes, others for very much longer periods of up to fourteen or fifteen minutes. Once children have lost interest in an activity and their attention has wandered, little or no more learning takes place. It is best to change an activity before children lose interest so that they are left wanting more and looking forward to the next opportunity to do the same activity. Over-exposure to an activity leads to boredom. As children develop, so their span of concentration lengthens. It is important not to confuse a child's span of concentration with his need to move physically (see page 14). The rest of this section considers key areas of development in the child that the teacher must be aware of, pointing to some of the important themes to consider.

LANGUAGE DEVELOPMENT

Language 1 development is a major subject in its own right. It is, however, important to realise that a child's ability to use his first language is a crucial factor in the learning process. The degree to which he can use Language 1 to communicate will reflect on his ability to acquire Language 2. Teachers need to know the level of Language 1 development of each child they teach. Where a child's Language 1 ability is not sufficiently developed, teachers can jointly plan activities common to Language 1 and the English lesson. They can also advise parents on suitable language experiences which should help improve the child's use of language (see Chapter 3).

COGNITIVE DEVELOPMENT

A child's language-learning skills are not isolated from the rest of his mental growth. It appears that concepts that he has learned in Language 1 can be transferred to Language 2 (see Section 2 of this Chapter).

Children find it easier if learning a new concept takes place in Language 1 rather than in Language 2. It is also easier for the person explaining the concept, as the child's use of Language 1 is more developed and thus explaining is easier. Teachers who have no other way but to explain in Language 2 will find it helpful to consult books that deal with introducing concepts to young children in a structured way. They also need to plan a longer learning programme, as children will need more experiences and time to learn a completely new concept. This is a particular problem in ESL situations (see Figure 3), where all teaching may be through the medium of English and not through the child's Language 1.

AGE	7–8
GROUP SIZE	35
BACKGROUND	Language 1 = Japanese; an EFL situation
SCHOOL	Japanese language primary school with regular English as a Foreign Language programme

In their English class, the children were given a xeroxed copy of a map of the world from their textbooks. They were then asked to copy details of countries taken from their textbooks on to it, and to colour in the countries. As the children had not begun to make plans or maps in their Japanese lessons, they were not ready to understand the concept of a map of the world and the activity degenerated into a colouring session. If the teacher had replaced the activity with another more suitable task (for example, making and colouring flags of the countries), the children would have been able to understand and use the related language more easily.

'Until a child is ready to take a particular step forward it is a waste of time to try and teach him to take it' (HMSO – The Plowden Report 1967). Teachers of young children are conscious that children reach a certain point when they are ready to learn something new. This 'readiness' stage is very clear in activities like numbers, reading and writing (see Dunn 1984: Chapters 1 and

2). If a child is asked to learn a certain skill before he is ready, he cannot do it (see the above inset). This failure results in disappointment and sometimes loss of interest. It is, therefore, very important for a teacher to be able to recognise children's 'readiness' to learn a certain concept and make use of the enthusiasm that often accompanies it.

Teachers also need to know what concepts children in their class already know and what concepts they are likely to learn during the school year. Some textbooks for learning English include concepts which are too difficult for young children. Where teachers are faced with this type of problem, they can substitute different activities which are right for the developmental age of the child and at the same time give the same language experience.

Since the individual differences and especially cognitive differences between young children of the same age are so great, to teach a class as one unit does not give a child the individual attention he needs. Where classes are very large, teachers can divide the children into small groups and within each group give them individual attention. However, young children until about the age of eight are still dependent on adult support for much of what they do. This is especially so in the English classroom and although they may work in groups their relationship still has to be with the teacher. Only when they are older are they ready to have less contact with the teacher and relate more with the group leader.

It is essential to be able to judge how much new material children can absorb at one time. The amount that they are capable of taking in depends on their developmental level, enthusiasm, interest and on the teacher's skill in presenting the material. It also depends on a factor that is often overlooked: the class's mood. Children are excitable; snow or heavy rain, a birthday to be celebrated or an approaching festival can excite them. If they are excited they cannot concentrate for as long as usual. Mood is infectious; if one or two children are excited, this can spread to the rest of the class. When a class is in such a mood, they generally do not want to settle down to quiet activities. In this case it is better not to force the children, but to leave the quiet activities until the next lesson when things have usually got back to normal.

Some teachers worry that they may be making young children work too hard. If a child is learning by taking part in activities, it seems to be impossible to push him further than he wants to go. Once he has reached saturation point, he 'switches off' his interest; he no longer concentrates on what he is doing and lets his mind, and in some cases even his body, wander to other activities. However hard a teacher tries to attract his attention back to the original activity, once he has 'switched off', she is not successful.

It is impossible for children to learn everything perfectly in each lesson. For this reason part of every lesson should consist of going over previous work (remedial work) to help children to consolidate the language and the concepts they have been exposed to. Failure to consolidate any one stage of learning affects the next stage of learning. If new activities are presented before sufficient consolidation of previous activities has taken place, a gradual accumulation of things not properly understood begins to grow. This often leads to a feeling of 'not being good' at English.

On the other hand, activities which are right for the stage of development and are properly consolidated give a feeling of being successful, which in turn motivates. If children can go from one successful activity to another, motivation takes place naturally.

EMOTIONAL DEVELOPMENT

It is difficult to examine all aspects of a child's emotional development. However, teachers should be aware that young children differ in temperament. Some children are aggressive, others shy, some are over-anxious to please and in some cases frightened of making a mistake; others are moody, especially if they do not get what they want. Temperament affects their ability to take part in language-learning activities. Teachers need to be aware of differences in temperament and be able to help children make the best of an activity. By watching children in the classroom, in the playground or with their parents and by talking to parents about their children, teachers can gradually find out about children's temperaments. Once a teacher knows what sort of temperament a child has, she can allocate particular activities to him which give him an opportunity to develop his character. She also knows better when to give praise and encouragement.

PHYSICAL DEVELOPMENT

Not only cognitive development but also physical development plays an important role in determining what activities are right for the young child. 'Patterns of physical growth tend to be broadly similar for all children. As coarse muscle control becomes finer, a child can make more complex and differentiated movements' (Tucker 1977: 42).

Muscular development affects a child's ability to focus his eyes on a page, line or word – a prerequisite for reading. It also affects his ability to hold a pencil, a pair of scissors or a paint brush. Before a child has developed a certain degree of muscular control, some activities are too difficult for him.

Teachers often complain that young children have difficulty in sitting still. They want to move, to wriggle and touch everything. To quote Millar, 'The fact that children find it less easy than adults to sit still for long periods, not to bang their heels against a chair, not to jump up, or move their arms, or touch objects, to execute fine movements with their fingers and modulate their voices, is not a question of having more energy to spill, but of comparative lack of integration and control of movement systems' (in Tucker 1977: 21). Activities need to give children an opportunity to move around within the classroom. Rhymes, for example, can include activities like jumping or dancing, and games can include physical activity games. In many cases the need to wriggle and move might look like a loss of interest, but if the activity is right for the child, the child will still be involved and listening even if he is wriggling.

The debate continues as to whether there are biological differences between young boys and girls which make them behave differently or whether the differences are developed by their way of life and education. The conclusion of the Plowden Report was that 'boys and girls develop at different rates and react in different ways'. In some societies it is a fact that young boys' performance is very different from that of young girls. For example, in societies where the young boy plays most of his time at home and is hardly disciplined, while the young girl is expected to help in the house, especially with the cooking, the difference in behaviour, physical control of muscles and all-round maturity of girls and boys is very great. The young girls generally have finer control of their fingers and hands which shows up in activities involving writing and colouring.

'Boys' hearing ability appears to develop later than girls' (Goodacre: 10). This can affect their ability to read aloud. Early childhood illnesses, such as middle ear infections, can leave some damage which may go undetected in Language 1, because hearing has been partially replaced by lip-reading. Hearing disabilities may only show up when learning another language.

Children aged six sometimes have some pain and general malaise caused by the cutting of their six-year molar teeth. This may make them slightly moody and less able to settle down and concentrate. Around seven or eight years old, children lose their top and bottom front teeth, which is embarrassing for many and makes pronunciation difficult. During this period it is better not to make children work orally by themselves; if they work in small groups, their temporary sub-standard pronunciation is less noticeable. Similar considerations apply to children fitted with an orthodontic apparatus to straighten teeth.

1.4 Adult influence on children's language learning

'Personal relations appear to form the matrix within which a child's learning takes place' (Donaldson 1978: 88). A young beginner is entirely dependent on his teacher for all learning in the initial stages. The responsibility for his success is, to a large extent, in the hands of his teacher and how well she manages to build up a personal relationship with the child and his family (see Chapter 3). Through this personal relationship, attitudes to learning English and English culture appear to be transmitted from teacher to child. Thus, a teacher's enthusiasm and interest is often contagious.

Young children are eager to build up a relationship with their teacher. They are not inhibited or shy if they feel at ease with her and secure in the atmosphere of the classroom. To build up a personal relationship, children have to feel the teacher respects them and understands their needs; they, on the other hand, have to feel a respect for their teacher. To understand the children she teaches, a teacher not only has to understand their developmental needs, but also has to be able to be on their level and see things through their eyes.

Young children are dependent on the teacher for input of language and for organising language-acquisition activities. In the classroom where only English is used, children depend on the teacher in the initial stages for all interpersonal communication; she is usually the only English speaker. It is up to her to sustain this communication and develop and extend it. Through careful planning she can ensure the children's success and give the encouragement and praise necessary to motivate them.

Research shows that parents and the home are the strongest influence on a child's life. If parents are interested in their children's achievements in English and show appreciation of their successes, the children will be motivated. What parents think and say about what a child is doing and achieving is important to the child. A child wants to please his parents and is happy when they become involved in what he is doing.

Many parents are eager to know what is going on in the English lesson and some want to help in the teaching by listening to cassettes with their children at home (see Chapter 3). It is important to sustain this interest and enthusiasm as, apart from motivating, it helps to consolidate. It also gives an added opportunity for interpersonal communication in both Language 1 and Language 2. Children without parental support are undoubtedly at a disadvantage.

1.5 Cultural influence on language development

Although young children pass through the same stages of development, it is important to realise the influence that a child's society and culture can have on his development. It is especially important for native speaker teachers working overseas to be aware of a child's role at home and in society. To expect young beginners, whose home life is very different from a western home, to respond to material and activities in the classroom like an American, Australian or English child of the same age is not realistic. Even the type of teaching in other lessons at school and the relations with other teachers will influence a child's behaviour in the English class. If, in some lessons, the child is taught by very formal methods and a distant, authoritarian teacher, he will have difficulty responding initially to a progressive, informal style of teaching. Without adequate knowledge of the child's background, it is difficult to understand fully his behaviour in the classroom or to plan the right type of activities from which he can benefit.

2 Fitting the syllabus to the child

When preparing a syllabus for young beginners, it is important to have a clear idea of what the programme aims to achieve. In the words of Hawkes, 'age, cultural context and general educational priorities influence content more than purely linguistic considerations' (Hawkes 1981: 33). Many experienced teachers of young children have been aware for a long time that purely linguistically based programmes are not successful with young beginners and have supplemented courses with their own material which caters more closely for the child's developmental level, needs and interests. On the other hand, programmes which are based entirely on the needs and interests of the child, without any linguistic considerations underlying the syllabus design, tend to be haphazard and less effective than those which have the guidance of a linguistic programme designed for young beginners.

2.1 A beginner's syllabus

Young children learning English in schools or classes can be divided into three main groups:

1 English as a Foreign Language (EFL)
2 English as a Second Language (ESL)
3 Bilingual

Figure 3 gives a very general outline based on the way schools and

Figure 3 A general outline of English Language Teaching (ELT)

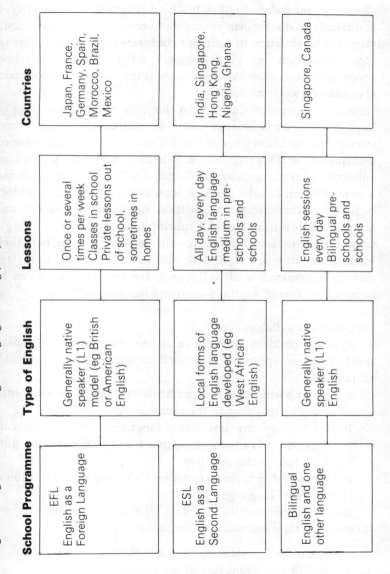

School Programme	Type of English	Lessons	Countries
EFL English as a Foreign Language	Generally native speaker (L1) model (eg British or American English)	Once or several times per week Classes in school Private lessons out of school, sometimes in homes	Japan, France, Germany, Spain, Morocco, Brazil, Mexico
ESL English as a Second Language	Local forms of English language developed (eg West African English)	All day, every day English language medium in pre-schools and schools	India, Singapore, Hong Kong, Nigeria, Ghana
Bilingual English and one other language	Generally native speaker (L1) English	English sessions every day Bilingual pre-schools and schools	Singapore, Canada

Fitting the syllabus to the child   19

classes organise their English teaching programmes. In reality, it is difficult to distinguish clearly between EFL, ESL or bilingual classes. The situation in different countries is continually changing, and within any given country different types of school programmes can exist. For these reasons the examples of countries given are general and can alter.

Most EFL beginners start from the same point of knowing no English or just a few isolated words. By contrast, ESL learners may start with some knowledge of English as it may be used at home on occasions or on TV programmes. Whatever their background, all children need to acquire sufficient English for interpersonal communication to take place as soon as possible. Once children begin to communicate, acquisition takes place quickly and naturally. The initial stage of acquiring sufficient English to begin communicating is common to all beginners, whether their learning situation is EFL, ESL or bilingual. This initial first stage should be common to all syllabuses. For convenience it can be termed Part One of a child's language-learning syllabus.

Part One of a syllabus aims:
1   to equip children with the means to communicate at a basic level in simple spoken and/or written language in predictable situations
    a   by exposing them to prefabricated language with little creative language in the initial stages
    b   by leaving any unsuitable language, for example conceptually too advanced or structurally too complex, until Part Two of the syllabus
    c   by exposing them to constant recycling and repetition of the same language
2   to enable children to talk and write at a basic level about themselves, their immediate surroundings and interests.

The length of time it takes to complete Part One depends on:
1   the length and frequency of the exposure to English

2 the age of the children
3 the type of schooling in Language 1
4 the quality of teacher and materials
5 the number of pupils in the class.

Once Part One has been completed, children are ready to follow a syllabus based on the needs of an EFL, ESL or bilingual programme (Part Two). At the same time, they are ready to recycle Part One at a linguistically and cognitively more advanced level.

ADAPTING A SYLLABUS

Existing syllabuses can be adapted to make Part One and Part Two. The following are some examples of adaptations which have been made.

1 **Changing the order of the introduction of material**
   a Introducing prefabricated language in the first lessons
      Young beginners quickly and easily acquire prefabricated language. This is particularly so in the case of rhymes (see Chapter 5). To help children progress quickly and use English, more prefabricated language can be included in the first lessons and in the early stage of Part One than in the average Language 1 classroom for children of the same age.
   b Reducing the amount of vocabulary
      A young beginner needs only a basic minimum of words to begin to communicate. For this reason, many items of vocabulary can be left until later in Part One when children have greater oral ability and can therefore acquire new language more easily.
2 **Introducing additional activities**
The syllabus often does not give sufficient opportunities for children's acquisition needs. If activities which are right for children's interests and developmental level are 'stage managed' in the classroom, the children are stimulated and, providing they

have the linguistic tools, they will communicate. In some cases they are so stimulated that if they have not got the linguistic tools, they communicate using half English and half Language 1. This was so in the case of a little French boy who shouted, 'J'ai twenty!' in a game.

3 Increasing the opportunities to talk about children's immediate interests

Children want to talk in English about the same things they talk about in Language 1. Although they do not have sufficient English to talk about things at the same level or in such detail, activities can be selected which are more or less parallel to those in the Language 1 classroom. A good syllabus follows children's interests; where a set syllabus introduces items which are beyond children's present interests, these items can be left until the end of Part One or until Part Two when children have greater oral ability and are more conceptually mature. At this stage local cultural content can be extended to learning about customs, daily life and festivals in English speaking countries. Without some inclusion of cultural information about English-speaking countries, problems in communication and understanding can arise. Young children begin school with few fixed ideas and prejudices and 'a second language programme which teaches cultural information along with language can produce a more tolerant, less prejudiced child' (Donoghue and Kunkle 1979: 9).

2.2 The syllabus and the textbook

Many teachers may not be involved in syllabus design and may not have any choice in the textbook they are provided with. However, they need to understand the underlying principles of the syllabus in order to use the textbook effectively and adapt it to their own situations.

Some teachers find that they are presented with textbooks

which they are expected to complete by a certain date. Few are ideal for young beginners, as many are written for international use, yet each country and each individual classroom is different in its needs. However, with adaptations and additions of activities and materials, teachers can manage to make them fit the needs of the children they teach.

ADAPTING A TEXTBOOK
When adapting a textbook, the teacher may find the following suggestions useful:

1 Oral introduction
Young children find it easier to learn from real objects than from pictures in books. Where the oral introduction in the textbook illustrates objects common to any classroom (pens, pencils, etc), children find a lesson easier to understand if real pens and pencils are substituted. This also allows the teacher to grade more flexibly the presentation of new vocabulary.

2 Speed of introduction of material
Children find it easier to learn one concept at a time. Where a page in a book presents children with a confusing amount of material, it is better to take one item from the page and deal with it, if possible, by relating it to children's personal experience. For example, a page in one textbook introduces *my father*, *my mother*, *my sister* and *my brother* and then *Mr* and *Mrs*, all referring to the child in the textbook. This is best divided into two steps, which are initially taught by relating the language to the children's own families.

3 Simplifying too complex material
Methodological techniques need introduction and adult methods of coding language are often too complex for young beginners. For example, where textbooks include substitution tables, teachers can introduce the language orally in activities. Once the children are familiar with the language, they can use it orally in games and

read it from flash cards. By this time they should be very familiar with the language and, under the guidance of the teacher, be able to use a substitution table.

4 Supplementing the text

A text may be culturally too far removed from children's experience for them to be able to interpret the photographs or pictures meaningfully. This is particularly so in the case of texts prepared for the European primary schools; children with a completely different life style, for example in the Middle East, have difficulty in relating to them. In such a case a teacher may find it helpful to transpose the activities in the book to the children's own society, thus making them more meaningful. It is also very common to find books which introduce too much vocabulary on one page for young beginners to absorb at once. Teachers can find ways of introducing the vocabulary orally in steps and later on flash cards before children are asked to read the page. Consolidation can take place by playing *What's This?*, *Memory Game*, *Snap* and *Bingo* using the items of vocabulary (see Dunn 1984: Chapter 1).

5 Introducing and consolidating reading

Children sometimes find difficulty in remembering prepositions such as: in front of, beside, near, behind, etc. Before reading them in the textbook, the teacher can introduce them orally and follow this by showing them on flash cards. She can follow this up by holding up a flash card with the word 'near' on it and adding orally 'the blackboard'. One of the class must then go to the place indicated. A workbook activity may serve as a good way of consolidating reading, for example following instructions on how to colour a picture. The author's *Developing English with young learners* looks into this subject in much greater detail.

6 Supplementing handwriting practice

Only one example and a short practice exercise for learning each letter of the alphabet may be insufficient for very young children or children learning a new script. Where a textbook gives insufficient practice, teachers can help consolidate by using writing patterns (see Dunn 1984: Chapter 2).

Teachers need to think carefully about:

a where their textbook material needs supplementing
b how to supplement their textbook material
c how best to present their textbook material.

Teachers' books may have some useful suggestions. It is profitable as well as economical in terms of time and effort to work in groups. School groups and English club groups can meet to discuss experiences and build a pool of resources and materials.

3 Planning lessons

Children appear to learn more easily when they know what to expect in a lesson and what the teacher expects of them. Apart from making them feel more secure, it gives them confidence. It also enables them to predict situations and the language likely to be used in them.

For this reason, teachers often find it helpful to use the same lesson framework for each lesson. This framework is the basis of a routine which is followed in each lesson, the activities being slotted into the framework. After a few lessons children get to know the routine and often feel so 'at home' that they move on to the next stage of a lesson, making the preparations themselves even before the teacher has given any instructions (see Figure 4).

The security of knowing what comes next enables young children to concentrate on the activity in which they are involved, free from the worry that they will not understand what to do next. The calmness of a class that is used to a routine is quite noticeable, especially when compared with a class haphazardly planned with little or no regular routine.

3.1 Lesson framework

The lesson framework (Figure 4) is very basic and can be modified to fit different teaching situations by altering the duration of the three phases. The time spent on each phase can also be altered from lesson to lesson to fit in with the aims of the lesson, the

Phase	Aim	Activities	Place
Introduction			
Phase One *Class activities* Whole class involved in the same activity; all together, in groups or in pairs	Revision of previous activities Teaching new language Explanation of individual activities, through reading, writing, handwork, to be consolidated in Phase Two	Rhymes, songs, finger plays, games and story telling	Sitting informally on the floor round the teacher if at all possible
Phase Two *Individual activities* Working as individuals or in groups	Consolidating language previously experienced Completing activities at own level and speed	Reading, writing, spelling, colouring, handwork	Sitting in own desk or at a table
Phase Three *Class activities* Whole class involved in the same activity, working in a class or in groups	Further consolidating experiences	Acting, puppets, language games of various types	In an open space or sitting in groups
Ending			

children's development and attention span, as well as their particular needs.

BEGINNING AND ENDING A LESSON OR SESSION
The social function of greeting people and saying goodbye, although limited linguistically, allows the teacher to have personal contact with each individual child at the beginning and end of each lesson. An experienced teacher uses this to sum up a child's mood at the beginning of the lesson and to add a few words of encouragement. At the end of a lesson she uses it to send him home with a few words of praise and a comment on his participation. Young children look forward to this special time with their teacher and her few words are very important to them; these words also play an important part in motivating (see Chapter 1, Section 4).

Phase One
Children sit informally on the floor on a mat round the teacher, who sits on a chair slightly elevated so that the children can see her face and especially her mouth. Phase One begins by revision of rhymes, songs, etc in a type of 'warming-up' activity, which helps children get used to hearing, understanding and using English. Sitting close to the teacher like this enables children to see the teacher's mouth movements and hear clearly, which is essential for imitation and self correction. This initial revision period is followed by other oral activities; some introducing new language items and some revising familiar ones, which can involve the whole class, groups or pairs of children. This period is managed by the teacher. As the children get used to the teacher's way of working, they can take over some of the organising themselves.

Phase Two
Children sit at their own tables or desks and work in pairs, in

small groups or as individuals. Activities include colouring, reading and writing. This is a calm period. During Phase Two, the teacher goes round the class talking to the children in turn about the activities they are doing. The children get on at their own speed, working by themselves with occasional words of encouragement from the teacher to sustain their interest.

Phase Three

By the end of the lesson or session the children are getting tired. They become restless and often want to move around. Phase Three is planned to give children the opportunity to take part in games or activities which can include handwork and drama (see Dunn 1984: Chapter 4).

LENGTH OF LESSONS OR SESSIONS

The frequency and length of lessons is generally fixed by school programmes or local circumstances. Where teachers have some choice of fixing the length and frequency of lessons, the following points may be helpful. Lessons should neither be too short, for example twenty minutes for seven year old immigrant children in a British infant school; or too long, for example a pre-school class with an unplanned three-hour programme in Italy.

Lessons which are too short do not give children enough time to get 'warmed up' or for sufficient experiences to take place for adequate acquisition and consolidation. Lessons which are very long can be broken by a snack time after Phase Two, before leading on to Phase Three. Ideally lessons for seven year old children, for example, should last forty-five minutes and should be more frequent than once a week.

3.2 Classroom organisation

CLASS NUMBERS

Young children need to be treated as individuals by the teacher if optimum learning is to take place. For this reason classes should not be too big. The ideal number seems to be somewhere between twelve and twenty. Classes that are too small are also not ideal for learning. Too few children makes it difficult to play some games and there is less interpersonal communication.

Some teachers, however, are faced with classes of more than forty young beginners. It is possible to organise large classes in the way suggested in Figure 4, but children have to work in pairs or groups instead of individually. This takes careful preparation and organisation. It also entails training children to work in groups, unless they are already working in this way in other lessons.

EQUIPMENT AND LAYOUT

Atmosphere is important for children and if teachers expect them to use only English in the lesson, children need as much help as possible to make the transition from Language 1. It is possible to create an English atmosphere in a classroom with pictures, posters, notices and books in English or by playing English songs on a cassette.

The 'warming-up' period at the beginning of Phase One also helps to create an atmosphere and get children into the mood for using English. Where the classroom is used for other subjects and it is not possible to keep English pictures, etc on the wall from lesson to lesson, or where children use the same room with the same teacher for Language 1, teachers find it a good idea to have a portable teacher's kit of English things. The experience for children of unpacking the kit at the beginning of the lesson with the teacher and putting it away at the end of the lesson is an added opportunity for interpersonal communication.

If children are going to take part in real-life activities in the classroom, furniture has to be arranged to allow this to take place. Furniture has also to be arranged to allow for maximum communication between children. Desks in straight rows have to be grouped together so that a child can talk to the child next to him or across the table to other children. A great number of teachers are faced with far from ideal classrooms, such as small rooms equipped for adults with lecture chairs, a desk and writing board. But with a little enterprise and furniture moving, the worst situation can generally be improved sufficiently for some activities to take place. This can begin by pushing the teacher's desk into a corner and using it to store equipment.

Basic needs for a young beginner's classroom (see Figure 5) are listed below.

1   An area, possibly a corner, where children can sit on a mat or carpet round the teacher's chair for Rhyme Time in Phase One.

2   Desks or tables to provide a flat top for writing, or handwork. These can be pushed together for group work or to provide a bigger surface. Some children find sloping surfaces difficult to work on.

3   An area in which to play games, act, etc. Desks and tables can be pushed aside to make this area.

4   A blackboard or whiteboard or equivalent, low enough for children to read from it and write on it. Many boards are too high for young children.

5   An exhibition area for pictures, homework, etc. Where there is no wall board, it is possible to prop workbooks up on window or blackboard ledges at the end of a lesson. Portable kits can include display boards or cloths on which to pin pictures.

6   Equipment for handwork including crayons, round-ended scissors, paste, staplers, etc. This can be stored in labelled containers easily accessible and easily tidied. (Labels give reading practice.)

7   Where possible classrooms should have a cassette recorder to provide listening experiences. This should be kept on some flat surface away from blackboard chalk dust.

8   Ideally a classroom should have a book corner (see Dunn 1984: Chapter 5).

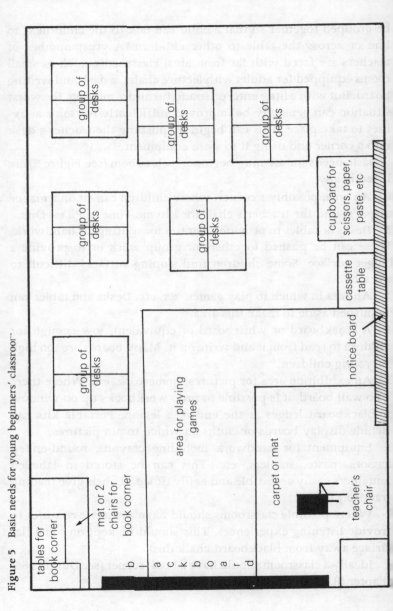

Figure 5 Basic needs for young beginners' classroom

- group of desks
- group of desks
- group of desks
- group of desks
- group of desks
- cupboard for scissors, paper, paste, etc
- cassette table
- notice board
- area for playing games
- blackboard
- carpet or mat
- teacher's chair
- mat or 2 chairs for book corner
- tables for book corner

3.3 Planning activities

Teachers should not expect language acquisition activities to take place spontaneously in the classroom. Activities have to be planned before the lesson to fit with children's developmental needs and interests. It is important that they should lead on from previous activities, and should give ample opportunity for repetition and transfer of old and new language items. See the following examples of how to plan a series of activities.

AGE	6–8 years
GROUP SIZE	10
BACKGROUND	2 children Language 1 = English
	8 children Language 1 = French
SCHOOL	French language primary school
	Private EFL class outside school hours

The teacher began by revising the names of the colours by showing demonstration cards. Using the same cards she then played *What's this?* (see Dunn 1984: Chapter 1). The teacher then gave each child a card with a shape outlined on it, which the children were asked to colour red. As each child finished colouring the card, he brought it up to the teacher who asked him 'What's this?' The teacher then gave the child a second card and asked him to colour it blue. The activity continued until each child had a red, blue, green and brown card. The teacher then divided the children into pairs to play *Matching* or *What's this?* using their own words.

FREQUENCY OF ACTIVITIES

For maximum acquisition the same activity needs to take place at least twice on two different occasions. It seems that the first time an activity takes place, children do not acquire the maximum input, even if they are familiar with a similar type of activity in Language 1, as they are partially occupied in working out what is going on. The second time the same activity takes place they are already familiar with it and can concentrate more on talking about it. This is very noticeable in handwork activities. Some activities may stretch over several lessons. In these cases language input needs to be carefully planned to make sure the children gain the maximum benefit from the activity.

VARIETY OF ACTIVITIES

Within a lesson there should be a variety of activities, some of which are familiar to the children, others new. Familiar activities give opportunities to revise, consolidate and expand on language items. New activities should offer a challenge and require some effort. Without an effort, children have no feeling of satisfaction, but where an activity is too difficult they quickly lose interest and feel they have failed.

No lesson should consist of more new experiences than familiar ones as this would be too confusing for children who seem to thrive on the security of knowing what to expect next.

INTEGRATING ACTIVITIES

A good activity is naturally integrated. Within it, the skills of listening, speaking, reading and writing are undifferentiated, if children are sufficiently mature (see Dunn 1984: Chapter 4). Activities should be planned to fit into the framework of the lesson. An activity may begin in Phase One of the lesson and be continued in Phase Two. Other activities may be continued through the three stages of the lesson but for different lengths of time.

The time planned to be spent on different activities often has to be modified on the actual day to fit in with the children's mood and span of concentration. If an activity is being done by all the class and about one third of the children lose interest, it is time to

AGE	7–8 years
GROUP SIZE	18
BACKGROUND	Language 1 = French; an EFL situation
SCHOOL	French language primary school
	Private EFL class outside school hours

Throughout the lesson activities were planned using language connected with time

Phase One	Revision of the rhyme and using it as a game
	Tick tock tick tock
	Listen to the clock
	Tick tock tick tock
	Listen to the clock
	One two three four five
	What time is it?
	Five o'clock (Dunn 1979: 15)
Phase Two	Handwork making clocks. Either cutting out clocks and hands from cardboard, or drawing different types of clocks and watches showing different times in exercise books
Phase Three	Playing the game *What's the time, Mr Wolf?* (see Chapter 5)

change to some other activity. Children's attention can often be held by asking different children in turn to take part in an activity (for example, reading, singing or playing a game). The suspense of waiting for a turn excites children and holds their attention. Whilst waiting for a turn and listening to others, some language acquisition seems to take place. When a class is very excited, it is better to shorten the time spent on quiet activities in Phase Two and spend more time on physical activities in Phase Three of the lesson.

Throughout a lesson it is essential to keep up a momemtum by changing activities if children are to be involved for the maximum length of time in some language acquisition activity. To help do this and switch smoothly from one activity to another, some teachers slip a card into their watch strap on which they write the order of activities. In this way they do not lose time in having to look at their lesson notes to find out what is planned next.

ORGANISING ACTIVITIES
According to the size of the class, activities can be for:

    all the class
    boys/girls
    groups/pairs/individuals
    younger and older
    readers/non-readers
    writers/non-writers.

Children should be encouraged to help each other. They appear to consolidate their own knowledge through teaching someone else and it is a good exercise in communication. Older children can help younger children, quicker children can help slower ones, readers can help non-readers and so on. Other children from higher classes can be invited to take part in activities like plays. English-speaking visitors should also be invited and recruited to contribute to activities.

In some activities that are planned for the whole class the situation can arise where the quick children always answer first or win, giving the slower children little or no opportunity to practise language. In these cases the quick children can be asked to organise the game or take some organising responsibility, thus removing them from actually playing the game and so giving the slower children a chance.

Other activities can be organised for groups or pairs (for example, reading, handwork and playing games). However, unless children are used to working with other children, they may be unable to benefit from a group situation. Some young children are not ready to work with other children and, although they are placed in groups or pairs, they continue to get on with their own individual task. In these cases they should be allowed to continue as individuals. In time, they will probably join in naturally.

If possible, all work achieved in a lesson should be shown to the rest of the class and discussed with them. This can be done by a quick exhibition at the end of a lesson when work is displayed in some corner of the classroom or even on the blackboard ledge. It can also be done at the beginning of the next lesson during Phase One when the children are gathered round the teacher. The teacher can hold up each book in turn and make some comment. A permanent exhibition of work can be displayed on the classroom wall, though for this to be of any value it should be changed quite frequently.

3.4 Making a lesson plan

Many teachers find it useful to break a syllabus into smaller units or schemes of work so that they have a clearer idea of what they should have achieved at the end of a term or month. It also helps in planning individual lessons. An example of a scheme of work designed to last a month is given in Figure 6.

It is essential to plan lessons carefully if children are to make progress from lesson to lesson. It is also necessary to plan more activities than may be needed in any one lesson, just in case children are not in a mood to work individually at some quieter activity or do not seem in the mood to do one of the planned activities. Teachers will find it useful to record any new ideas for

Figure 6 Scheme of work

AGE 7
GROUP SIZE 35

BACKGROUND Language1=French or Arabic
CLASS EFL class   2 lessons per week   50 minutes

Step	Identifying	Oral	Reading	Consolidation
1	Numbers 1–10		Arabic number flash cards	Game *How Many?* (see Chapter 5)
2	10 animals eg a dog/a cat	picture	flash card	Game *What's This? Bingo*
3	10 classroom objects, eg a book/a pencil	picture	flash card	Game *What's This? Bingo*
4	10 objects or animals with *an*, eg an elephant/an ant/an orange/an apple	picture	flash card	Game *What's This? Bingo*
5	joining 2 different objects already introduced with *and*, eg a dog and a cat	2 pictures	word flash cards joined with *and*	*Memory game* 'a dog and a cat'

Step	Identifying	Oral	Reading	Consolidation
6	plurals: 2 objects already introduced ending in /s/, eg two cats	2 pictures Poem: 1 cat, 2 cats (see Figure 13)	new flash cards	*Memory game* 'two cats'
7	plurals: 2 objects already introduced ending in /z/, eg two boys	2 pictures Poem: 1 boy, 2 boys Song (see Figure 15)	flash cards	*Memory game Snap* using /s/ and /z/ plurals
8	plurals: 2 objects already introduced ending in /ɪz/, eg two matches	2 pictures Poem: 1 match, 2 matches	flash cards	*Memory game Snap* using /s/ /z/ and /ɪz/

Notes

a) The steps are graded and can overlap, for example in consolidation work.

b) Steps can last for several lessons. Length of time to complete a step depends on the progress in a lesson. This scheme of work is planned to last a month.

c) Instructions for the games are given in Dunn 1984: Chapter 1.

activities or games in a book to which they can refer when looking for new ideas (see Chapter 5).

The example lesson plan given in Figure 7 brings together the points made in this Chapter. This plan is written out in full; most teachers develop their own quick way of recording. Other useful plans can be found in the Schools Council handbook (1969).

FOLLOW-UP NOTES

Follow-up notes are best completed directly after the lesson as details of what exactly happened during the lesson soon fade. The right-hand side of the lesson plan can be left for follow-up notes (see Figure 7). Follow-up notes form the basis from which the next lesson's plan is made. Follow-up notes should include:
- points to be consolidated in the next lesson
- language to be used in the next lesson
- activities to be repeated or extended
- new ideas to be included.

MONITORING CHILDREN

A list of children in the class should record absences but also note which children did not have adequate opportunity to speak or read during the lesson. This list helps the teacher to see at the beginning of the next lesson which children need extra opportunities. Unless the teacher records this type of observation, it is quite possible for a shy or quiet child to go from lesson to lesson using little English.

In some part of their lesson plan file, teachers should keep more detailed notes on individual children, their home background, their parents' knowledge of English, their general school progress in Language 1 and their progress or difficulties in English. This information should be regularly up-dated. A few minutes spent on simple quick monitoring directly after the lesson is more valuable for both the teacher and the child than once-a-term monitoring at the end of the term or for the Parents' Evening.

3.5 Linking home and school in lesson planning

Home and school are closely linked in the young child's mind and activities in the classroom should in some ways reflect what the child does or talks about at home, for example new additions to the family, pets or bicycles.

Most parents of young children are interested in knowing exactly what goes on in the lesson and teachers generally find that parents appreciate being informed or invited to informal class functions. Parents can be kept in touch in the following ways:

1   A parent's notebook in which the teacher writes information in the parent's Language 1 and the parent replies in writing in the notebook. This is a good way of keeping parents who do not understand English informed.

2   Notes written jointly by the teacher and children asking parents to come to a play, read a rhyme together with children or listen to a certain part of a cassette recording.

3   A special time once a month when parents come into the classroom to fetch their children and see a small exhibition of work.

4   An end-of-term concert. Parents who speak English can be asked to help in turns by the teacher or be asked to come on special days like birthdays to help with the snack. There is no reason why parents who do not speak English cannot help their children. However, the teacher needs to explain to these parents how to help their children by listening to a cassette recording together or watching them whilst they copy a poem or make some writing patterns (see Dunn 1984: Chapter 2).

There is often a considerable difference between the achievement of children who have parental support and children whose parents do not make any effort to help them or show little or no interest.

Figure 7 Lesson plan

Time 1hr * = equipment	Class 6b Age 7+ Lesson 4		
	LESSON	INPUT	FOLLOW-UP
Introduction 5 mins	Hello How are you? Hello	Fine, thank you	Pairs
Phase 1 20 mins	Rhyme Time REVISE 123 You can't see me 123 Clap with me Open/shut them NEW Tommy Thumb (2) Where are you? Here I am Here I am How are you? Fine, thank you	Stand up/Sit down Listen Again Do it again Hassan and Hamid Your turn Boys stand up Girls sit down Well done Good	Use puppet and draw eyes, nose, mouth Play 'Touch your nose, your mouth, your eye'
*	Revise Colours Red Black White Blue Brown Orange Green		
*	Flash cards 1-5 Numbers and words NEW 6,7,8 Numbers only	How many?	NEW 9,10
*	Identifying things a boy a girl a ball a tree a flower a cat a dog a monkey	What's this? - a boy, a girl etc	a pencil a book a rubber
	NEW a car a boat Quick game 'What's this?' Colours	What's this? red, blue etc	

* = equipment	LESSON	INPUT	FOLLOW-UP

Phase 2
10 mins
	Colouring picture cards for games *
	  a dog
	  a cat
	  a monkey
		Sit down
		Colour like this
		What's this? - a cat
		Point to a dog
			Begin introducing writing i/l
			Start card game with things 'What's this?'

Phase 3 20 mins	Quick games * 'What's this?' and * 'Where's the monkey?' (hiding toy monkey)	Your turn How many? Where's the monkey? Here Shut your eyes Count to 10 It's time to say goodbye	Play with new cards a dog etc
Ending 5 mins	Song Goodbye everyone (3), It's time to say goodbye		

Note
Instructions for the game *What's this?* are given in Dunn 1984: Chapter 1. Instructions for other games mentioned appear in Chapter 5

4 Beginning oral communication

'Primary level teaching materials are likely to be communicative in general character rather than building up a communicative competence by systematic steps' (Hawkes 1981: 33). Children acquire language by taking part in activities, and to take part in activities, they must want and need to communicate. The need to communicate in English is immediate and from the first lesson activities should take place in English.

When discussing how a four-year-old Chinese boy learned English, Krashen explained that 'Gestalt speech (prefabricated language) served as a short cut, a prefabricated tool to allow social interaction with a minimum of linguistic competence. Analytic (creative language) eventually predominated' (Krashen 1981: 91).

4.1 Using English from the start

In order for activities to take place in English, even from the first lesson, the teacher needs to rely heavily on prefabricated language for class organisation (see Chapter 2). Many activities and games, especially if the same or similar ones have taken place in the Language 1 classroom, have predictable language which can be picked up quickly. This language consists mainly of prefabricated routines. Examples can be found in Chapter 3 and Chapter 5.

Teachers, especially many non-native speaker teachers, are often amazed that lessons can be run using only English. They are equally surprised by the ease and speed with which young beginners can pick up and use quite long and complex phrases and sentences. To be able to run an all-English lesson, teachers need to organise and control activities more carefully than they would in a Language 1 classroom, so that the children have opportunities to use and repeat prefabricated language. With constant repetition of the same routines, children soon acquire the language involved and can begin to use it themselves to organise activities or games.

STARTING AN ACTIVITY
To start an activity the teacher can 'set the scene' by

a reviewing related activities done previously
b showing examples of work done by the children on previous occasions
c capturing the children's interest by explaining the new activity and showing them related material.

Checklist of language for starting an activity

Listen   Listen everyone   Are you ready?
                             Let's start
Say it with me
Do this like me
Copy me
Follow me
Have you got a pencil?   Have you got everything?
Has everyone got some paper?   Have you got some scissors?
Open your books at page five
Turn to page eight
Look at page five
Read it to me

Read this to me
Start here
Do the writing on page nine
Draw a . . .
Write this in your book
Copy this
Colour this
Colour this picture
Colour the picture on page six

SUSTAINING AN ACTIVITY

Checklist of language for sustaining an activity

Listen again
Say it again
John and Mary say it   Boys say it   Girls say it
Say it with them
Everyone say it again
Try it again
Now do this page   Now copy this   Now colour this
Read page five again   Read the next page
What are you doing?
What's this?
What colour is this?
What's he doing?   What's Sonia doing?
Where's the . . .

During an activity the teacher has to watch each child carefully, participating and helping and where necessary adding a comment to guide children or sustain their interest. Young children need to feel that the teacher knows what they are doing and that she is available so that they can show their work to her or discuss it with her. This close contact can only be achieved if the teacher moves round the classroom or sits in some place easily accessible to the children – for example, at one of their tables. To sit formally behind a desk creates a barrier for communication Some teachers take the opportunity whilst their class is colouring to move round to talk to individual children in a loud enough voice for all the others to hear and benefit from the use of the language. Others put on a cassette, for example a rhyme cassette, so that the children can listen to something whilst they colour and the teacher takes the opportunity to work in a corner of the classroom with a group who need some further consolidation.

ENDING AN ACTIVITY

Before putting things away at the end of an activity, it is a good idea for teachers to show the class what different children have achieved. As children gain oral fluency, they can show their work themselves and explain what they have done.

Checklist of language for ending an activity

Have you finished?   Has everyone finished?
Stop working   Stop writing
It's time to stop   Show me your book
Put away your things
Please put away the pencils   Put everything away
Please tidy up   Tidy the classroom
It's time to go home   It's time for the next lesson
Put your books in your bags   Put everything in your desk
Put your homework in your bag
Give your books to me   Give your pencils to Rebecca
Please collect the pencils   Please collect the crayons
Put the crayons on the table

The following list gives additional examples of prefabricated language which are useful in the classroom.

Language for socialising

Greetings
Hello
Hello everyone
Hello Anna
Hello   How are you?   I'm very well, thank you
I'm fine, thank you
Good morning   Good afternoon
Goodbye

Apologising
Excuse me   Excuse me, please
Sorry   I'm sorry
That's all right

Language for agreement/disagreement

Yes   Yes, that's right
No   No, try again, please

Language for praise

Good   Good, well done
Good work   Very good
That is very good writing   That's beautiful

4.2 Modifying language level for young beginners

'Perhaps we acquire by understanding language that is "a little beyond" our current level of competence. Optimal input includes structures that are "just beyond" the acquirers' current level of competence' (Krashen 1981: 102).

If the concepts in an activity have already been understood in Language 1, when the activity takes place in Language 2, young beginners can predict much of the meaning of the English used. To help in this, the language items used in the first lesson should be as simple as possible. Once children have understood these first language items and in some cases are capable of using them, the teacher can gradually expand them and introduce more complex language so that the language used is always 'just beyond' the children's level of understanding. This requires careful overall planning and schemes of work as well as careful planning from lesson to lesson.

To help in the initial stages of learning, language items can include words which identify colours, numbers, things in the classroom, self and personal items. In this way children have enough information to work out the gist of utterances referring to these things. In addition, facial gestures and gestures made with the hands, similar to the type of movements which accompany speech to very young children, can be exaggerated, especially in the first lessons, to help understanding.

In an acquisition-rich classroom, understanding by gist is going on all the time for all children at their own level of comprehension. However, it is wise to plan one or two new activities in each lesson which include understanding by gist. From lesson to lesson, gist experiences can be made progressively more complex, thus providing children with added input and at the same time increasing their skill in understanding by gist. Rhymes, story telling, news discussion, classroom and games management language all provide opportunities for this type of new language.

TRANSLATION

If young children understand that in the English lesson they are going to use only English, they are quite at ease and appear to enjoy the challenge of understanding and using English. For this reason it is a good idea to explain to children at the beginning of the first lesson that 'We are going to learn English by using it. This is an English classroom and in this room we use only English.'

To use only English with no translation or explanation in Language 1 needs careful planning of activities and adequate support of new material with visual aids, stories, rhymes and so on. Two other books in this series, *How to use games in language teaching* by Shelagh Rixon and *Look Here! Visual aids in language teaching* by Betty Morgan Bowen, contain many helpful suggestions. If teachers find that children have not understood the first time, they can repeat a second time or even a third time, adding a gesture or miming an action to help. Generally some children understand the first time and they often act as leaders for the other children.

In the very beginning stages some teachers may, when teaching a new concept, rhyme or story, feel it better to give a rough translation once quickly. In this case it is a good idea to use a different tone of voice so that children realise that it is not something which regularly happens in a lesson. Once children understand more English, teachers will find that it is no longer necessary to give a rough translation, providing they plan the new language items of their lesson material carefully. Young children do not expect a word for word translation; in fact many young children do not think of English being broken into words, each with a different meaning.

In the classroom children should be in an atmosphere where they are ready to communicate in English. Care should be taken to avoid breaking this atmosphere by translation or allowing the children to lapse into Language 1. If there is a short break or playtime half-way through the lesson and children go out into the playground, they immediately switch back into the language of the playground. When they return to the classroom after playtime, it is therefore necessary to get them back into the atmosphere and to use English. This takes time and effort. In such cases games in English can be organised during playtime. Where lessons are full of activities, a break, if required, can be taken in the form of a snack within the classroom. Where groups are small, children can take it in turn to bring a snack for every child. Snack-time gives a good opportunity to use social language in a real-life situation.

Habits of translating every new item the teacher says into Language 1 should be broken. It is possible to do this by playing games in which, for example, any child using Language 1 loses one of the ten points he has each lesson or has to stand up and turn round twice. If at the same time as introducing the game, the teacher takes care to use simpler language than usual and introduces no new language items for two or three lessons, the habit is fairly quickly broken. Once children get out of the habit of translating they seem to be pleased by their ability to use only English. They also seem to make quicker progress than before.

SIMPLIFICATION

It seems that children are subject to modified speech of some kind, no matter who is speaking to them' (Elliot 1981: 152). This type of speech, referred to as 'caretaker speech', is in the case of many beginners the only model of English they will hear. In the first lessons the teacher is in sole charge of the content of the lessons and any language interaction that might take place. Beginners at this stage are silent observers except for the repetition of rhymes or language items directed by the teacher.

The teacher's concern in the beginners' classroom is to ensure that activities can be organised and within these activities communication can take place. In order for communication to take place from the very first lesson, teachers need to modify their speech. Simple 'free conversation' is likely to fail as it will often not be understood.

AGE   5–6
GROUP SIZE   15
BACKGROUND   Language 1 = Japanese; an EFL situation
SCHOOL   Japanese language nursery school
                Private EFL class outside school hours

Lesson Plan (see Chapter 3)
Phase One of the lesson
The teacher held up a bag containing a toy monkey, car and boat and said, 'Look! A bag'. She then opened the bag so that the children could see inside and said, 'Look. What's in the bag?' A child replied, 'A car'. The teacher then said, 'Yes. A car's in the bag. Look again. What's in the bag?'. A child replied, 'A boat'. The teacher said, 'Yes. A boat's in the bag. Look. What's in the bag?'. A child saw the monkey and replied, 'A monkey'. The teacher pulled the monkey out of the bag and said, 'Yes. A monkey. A monkey', and as she said it, she had a game with the monkey jumping on the children in turn.

. . .

Phase Three of the lesson
The teacher plays either the game *Where's the monkey?* (see Chapter 5) in which she hides the toy monkey in the room or even in the bag, or the game *What's in the bag?* in which the children have to feel the one object in the bag and guess what it is.

Some teachers find it difficult in the initial stages to alter their 'free conversation' to simple language and are often surprised that children cannot understand their complex instructions. If communication is not taking place it is difficult to manage an activity-based lesson. To work out the right sort of language to use, teachers may find it useful to bear the following points in mind:

1 Children acquire structures in a relatively predictable order.
2 Situations in the classroom are controlled and give opportunities for the exaggerated use of prefabricated language, repetition, transfer and the recycling of language.
3 Techniques for suitable language can be copied from the way in which parents communicate with their children. This language, examined in detail by Elliot (1981), is often termed 'motherese'.

Once certain language items have been introduced and understood, the teacher can build on them from lesson to lesson, keeping routines and patterns 'just beyond' acquisition level. New items can be introduced:
  a by first using language with concrete objects or visual aids
  b by consolidating the language in an activity or game.

An example of this process can be seen in the above inset.

REPETITION

Repetition within an activity does not bore young children in the same way as it appears to bore older children and some adults. Repetition seems to give children a feeling of satisfaction and achievement which helps to motivate. They appear to enjoy doing the same thing again and again. When organising their own games in the playground, they choose to play the same games day after day.

TRANSFER

Language used in one part of a lesson can be transferred for use in another part of a lesson in a different activity. Complete items of language can be transferred or items can be transferred in part with, for example, the identifying word or words changed.

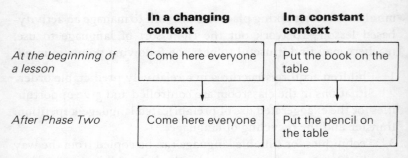

	In a changing context	In a constant context
At the beginning of a lesson	Come here everyone	Put the book on the table
After Phase Two	Come here everyone	Put the pencil on the table

By transferring language, teachers and children manage to use a small amount of familiar language for maximum communication. Young children who have not learned the technique of transferring are under-utilising their ability to communicate. By transfer the teacher helps children to get used to coping with different and unexpected situations in preparation for using English beyond the classroom.

CONSOLIDATION
For many children, meeting a language item once or twice is not sufficient for use. They need further opportunities to consolidate before they can use it. Teachers need to plan opportunities to consolidate language in each lesson. Consolidation may be in many forms – for example, games, a copying activity, repetition of a rhyme or repeating an activity. Some teachers are hesitant about repeating the same game or rhyme many times in case it may be boring. This seems to be an adult way of thinking; children enjoy repetition.

4.3 Creating methods of communication

DIALOGUE
In the first lesson, as the teacher is the only English speaker in the classroom, it is difficult to start language interaction. Adult learners from their experience have an idea of how to commu-

nicate in a foreign language and can work out some reply to a question from words they already know or have just learned. For young beginners, knowing how to build a conversation is beyond their experience, and before they can be expected to communicate, they have to be shown some examples.

In some cases there may be a child who has lived abroad and the teacher can work out some dialogues with him. Teachers can also arrange to borrow a child from an older class or invite an English-speaking parent to help for the first few lessons. Where a teacher has access to video cassettes, these can also be used to provide examples of dialogue. However, in all these cases the same problem exists. The teacher cannot control the replies to her questions and they may be too complex for this first stage of learning. For this reason, many teachers prefer to use a puppet whose language is controlled by the teacher.

From the first lesson the teacher can use the puppet to make simple dialogues which can initially be between the teacher and puppet and then between the teacher and child. Some teachers use two puppets, making them talk to each other without any 'human' taking part. This can be a useful variety of activity, but should not replace the teacher/puppet dialogue, as children appear to see themselves in the place of the puppet talking to the teacher or adult.

Teacher	Have you got a pencil?
Puppet	Yes, I have (*holding up a pencil*).
Teacher	Have you got a book?
Puppet	No, I haven't (*shaking his head*).
Teacher	Have you got a pencil?
Child	Yes, I have.
Teacher	Have you got a book?
Child	No, I haven't.

It is possible to build a whole world round a puppet, making it similar to a child in the class. For example, the puppet can have a school bag, can play the same games, have some small flash cards and so on. To do this, teachers and children will have to make a lot of the things themselves.

Teachers will find it a good idea to make simple puppets as an activity. Not only is making a puppet fun, but it provides opportunities for the use of language whilst making the puppet, as well as further opportunities for language practice once it is completed. Making a puppet can be done very quickly – the aim is not to produce a fine detailed piece of handwork, but something that can communicate. For this reason it is sufficient for a first puppet to be only a face or head (see Figure 8). During the year it is possible to make several types of puppets. The children enjoy repeating the activity and it gives the teacher a good opportunity to consolidate language as well as introduce new language in a familiar activity.

Figure 8   Easy-to-make puppets

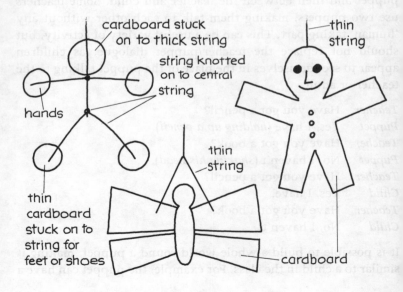

cardboard stuck on to thick string

string knotted on to central string

thin string

hands

thin string

thin cardboard stuck on to string for feet or shoes

cardboard

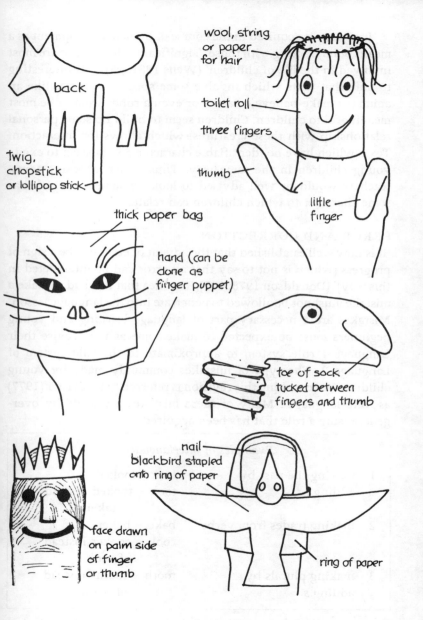

back

twig, chopstick or lollipop stick

wool, string or paper for hair

toilet roll

three fingers

thumb

little finger

thick paper bag

hand (can be done as finger puppet)

toe of sock tucked between fingers and thumb

nail

blackbird stapled onto ring of paper

ring of paper

face drawn on palm side of finger or thumb

'Language is acquired in the course of human development as a means of interacting with those "significant others" who are most involved in the life of children' (Wells 1981: 16). It is interesting to note that texts which involve some special character like an animal, a make-believe creature or even a robot seem to be most meaningful to children. Children seem to build up some personal relationship with these creatures, which allows for interaction. Texts which have no identifiable character do not seem to excite young children in the same way. Thus, when choosing texts, teachers would be well advised to look for material which has some character to which children can relate.

ERROR AND CORRECTION

'It is now well established that the advent of error can be a sign of progress (which is not to say that all error can be interpreted in this way)' (Donaldson 1978: 107). The idea that it is bad to make a mistake must not be allowed to penetrate into the language lesson. Mistakes are a necessary part of language learning and young beginners must be expected to make some as they revise their Language 1 rule system to approximate to the rule system of Language 2. The type of mistakes commonly made by young children when making this revision is referred to by Corder (1977) as 'interlanguage'. Many of these mistakes are made by over-generalising a rule that has been acquired.

Examples of interlanguage		
1	making the past by adding *ed*	look – looked took – tooked instead of taken
2	making trades from verbs	bake – baker cook – cooker instead of cook
3	making plurals by adding *s*	tooth – tooths instead of teeth

With more exposure to language, children revise their rule formation to incorporate the correct rule or exception.

When their children make interlanguage mistakes but the meaning has been understood, most parents make little comment or let the mistake pass without correction. Teachers are advised to do likewise, making sure the children have an opportunity soon after to hear the correct usage in some related activity. 'Correction has little value as children need to "learn by experience" and work out their own system. What a child works out for himself has quite a different status in his mind from what he is told by an authoritative adult' (Donaldson 1978: 108). For further information, see a book in this series devoted to learners' errors by John Norrish, *Language learners and their errors*.

4.4 Pronunciation

Young children have an enviable ability to pick up the sounds and patterns of language. Unlike most adolescents and adults, they do not need to be taught pronunciation. If the model speaker's pronunciation is good or they have access to recordings, and the children have opportunities to use language in real situations, they are capable of refining their pronunciation until in some cases it is hardly distinguishable from the model.

Mistakes in pronunciation need analysing carefully. In many cases they are not in individual sounds or clusters of sounds, but in the stress, rhythm or intonation of a single word, phrase or sentence. When the tune, as it is often called, is incorrect, what is said can be misunderstood and the feeling of the speaker misinterpreted.

There are differing opinions on the number of sounds which comprise English as well as their division into categories. The following simplified introduction is intended to help teachers when approaching a phonic reading programme. In any word with more than one syllable (a multi-syllabic word), one syllable has greater stress – that is, it is pronounced with greater strength – than others. The stress may be on the first syllable, as in *Mon*day, or in the second syllable, as in to*day*, or on the third syllable as in under*stand*. Within a phrase or sentence there is also a pattern of stressed and unstressed syllables. Many structural words pronounced in isolation are said in their strong form, but when they are said within a phrase or sentence, they take their weak form. Verbs are a good example of this. When teaching the verb *to be* a teacher stresses *am*, *is*, *are* and so on. But when these words appear in a phrase or sentence in normal fluent speech, weak or elided forms are usual. For example, 'He's in the playground and we're going out too'.

For these reasons, when teachers speak slowly to help children understand more easily, they need to take great care not to distort the pronunciation model by giving abnormal stress to words and by substituting strong forms for weak forms.

SOUNDS

The sounds of English (*phonemes*) are more numerous than letters of the alphabet (*graphemes*); and to help remember the sounds, teachers may find the phonetic alphabet, composed of forty-four symbols, useful (see Figure 9). This alphabet is based on what is called Received Pronunciation (RP), the accent used by the BBC Overseas Service. Much more detailed information on this subject is given in another book in this series (Tench 1981).

The vowels

The vowel sounds are not only made up of a e i o u. There are short and long vowels. If you say *bead* and *bid* to yourself, you will hear that the /i/ of *bead* is longer than the /ɪ/ of *bid*. Sounds made up of two vowels are called two-vowel dipthongs (for example /aʊ/ as in *house*) when both vowels are sounded in the same syllable. Watch out for confusing differences in terminology. The word

Vowel

/i/ as in bead	/ɜ/ as in bird	/ɪ/ as in bid	/ə/ as in cupboard
/e/ as in bed	/ɑɪ/ as in bide	/æ/ as in bad	/ɑʊ/ as in cowed
/ɑ/ as in bard	/eɪ/ as in paida	/ʌ/ as in bud	/əʊ/ as in bode
/ɔ/ as in bored	/ɔɪ/ as in boy	/ɒ/ as in pod	/ɪə/ as in beard
/ʊ/ as in good	/eə/ as in bared	/u/ as in booed	/ʊə/ as in poured

Consonant

/p/ as in pin	/tʃ/ as in cheer	/v/ as in vine
/t/ as in tin	/h/ as in hill	/ð/ as in this
/k/ as in coal	/l/ as in let	/z/ as in zeal
/m/ as in meal	/w/ as in wet	/ʒ/ as in measure
/f/ as in fine	/b/ as in bin	/dʒ/ as in jeer
/θ/ as in thin	/d/ as in din	/ŋ/ as in king
/s/ as in seal	/g/ as in goal	/r/ as in red
/ʃ/ as in ship	/n/ as in not	/j/ as in yet

Figure 9 The phonetic alphabet

'digraph' is an example. Some people use digraph to mean the orthographic *ai* in *sail* or *nail* (although this is pronounced as a dipthong /eɪ/). Some linguistic specialists define digraph more narrowly as two written vowel letters forming one unit, as in *amoeba* (where *oe* is actually pronounced /i/). Certain consonant combinations (such as *ch*) are also considered by some to be digraphs.

Consonants

There are many different ways to produce consonants. Consonants can be long or short. They can also be combined with semi-vowels (for example *news* /njuz/ and *queen* /kwin/). It is useful to note that there are many pairs of consonants which are made by using the mouth in exactly the same way, the difference being in whether they are voiced (that is the vocal chords vibrate and air passes through the larynx) or voiceless (the vocal chords do not vibrate). For example, /d/ is voiced and /t/ is unvoiced.

IMPROVING PRONUNCIATION

To help young children improve their pronunciation, teachers might find the following points useful.

1   Analyse the faults to find out if they are individual sound or pattern faults.

2   Based on the analysis of the faults, increase exposure to either patterns or sounds or both by:

   a   revising previous work

   b   introducing new rhymes or songs focusing on specific difficulties.

It is important to draw children's attention to mouth movements and to let them feel as well as hear the difference between voiced and voiceless sounds by putting their fingers on their throats.

3   Find out the difficulties that adult Language 1 speakers have in pronouncing English; for example, difficulties in pronouncing consonant clusters which are not present in Language 1, or in distinguishing between *r* and *l*. These difficulties may not be present in children's speech if the model has been good. If they are present, the exposure to a good model should be increased.

Many teachers are confused by the differences in representation between *phonetics* (the science of the analysis of speech sounds) and *phonics* – a method of teaching reading following the rules of speech sounds (phonemes) and letter (grapheme) relationship. The term 'phonics' was first used in the nineteenth century to refer to reading materials which helped children to read by learning the rules governing the sound/symbol relationship. During the last twenty years, new linguistic research has brought about a revision of phonic rules to bring them in line with more recent theories of linguistics.

5 Oral games, rhymes and songs for beginners

'Games are play activities that become institutionalised' (Garvie 1979: 101). They are in fact a form of play with rules. The rules which govern a game give it a form with a definite beginning and end. The rules ensure that the play takes more or less the same form each time. The consistency and predictability makes understanding easy for children as they know what is going to happen and what language is likely to be used. Young children seem to become absorbed in playing games which are appropriate for their stage of development and linguistic level without realising the meaningful and sometime drill-like repetitive use of language that games provide. Playing the same game over and over again seems to give young children a feeling of satisfaction as well as an opportunity to chance their luck and improve their skills, including linguistic skills.

However, not all games are suitable for young beginners and not all games give suitable language experience. Those played with no language participation are only time-fillers. Games are most useful if they are integrated with teaching, consolidating the use of language items.

5.1 Selecting games

Many games are not appropriate for young children as they require player participation which is too advanced for their stage of development. It is best to select games which have similar cognitive, physical and emotional levels to the games the children already play in Language 1. A short visit to a local playground is a quick way of getting this information.

Very young children enjoy cooperative games, for example *What's the time, Mr Wolf?* (see Section 5 of this Chapter), which involve the whole class and allow them to participate as much or as little as they feel able. Games which are based on individual competition to see who wins, or who gets the most cards, seem to be popular with children about seven years old or older. Children under seven sometimes find it difficult to lose. However, children get more experience in playing games and, especially with older children, they seem to grow to accept winning and losing, provided not too much importance is given to this. For many young children, having a turn in a game is more important than who actually wins. Chasing games in which there is a small element of fear excite young children, but the experience is only pleasurable if children know what to expect before it actually happens. In introducing chasing games it is advisable to explain the chase, without actually doing it the first few times the game is played. See the following inset for how this can be done.

AGE	6 to 7 years
GROUP SIZE	15
BACKGROUND	Language 1 = French
SCHOOL	French language primary school
	English EFL outside school hours

The teacher introduced a new game in which children skipped around Mr Bear who was in the middle of the circle pretending to look into a mirror to count his teeth. As they skipped they chanted,

How many teeth have you, Mr Bear?
How many teeth have you?
How many teeth have you, Mr Bear?
Can you tell me, please?

The children knew that when Mr Bear replied, 'One tooth' he would chase them and try to catch them before they reached the 'home'. If Mr Bear said any other number of teeth, for example, 'ten teeth', he would not chase them and they would have to ask him again. As this was the first time they played the game, the teacher played Mr Bear. She purposely did not say 'One tooth' until the third time, and then she let them run home without chasing them. However, the next time she chased them and caught a child who became Mr Bear.

Once children have learned to play a game or a type of game, they can concentrate on using the game language. Some games fit together with others in a series providing a natural sort of grading, for example, *What's this?* leads on to *Memory Game* and *Memory Game* to *Snap* and *Bingo* (see Dunn 1984: Chapter 5).

Children enjoy playing their own national games in English. Since children already know how to play these games, they have only to learn the linguistic labels in English. It is also interesting to teach games played by children in other countries, taking the opportunity to tell the children a little about the other country. There is a book called *Let's play Asian children's games*, published by the Asian Cultural Centre for UNESCO (1978) which gives some examples of games from other countries. In classes where there are immigrant children, it is a good idea to play games from their countries. The game, *Up and Down* (see Figure 10 below), is a good example of a starting game from Pakistan.

5.2 Language for games

When organising and managing games, the teacher needs to rely heavily on prefabricated language, especially language routines,

UP AND DOWN

A starting game to find a leader or the first to play

LEVEL Beginners
AGE Any age
PLAYERS Three
TIMING 2 to 3 minutes
LOCATION Inside/Outside
MATERIALS None

Aural/Oral
GAME LANGUAGE
One, two, three, four, five
This is 'up' This is 'down'
You are the leader
You are the first to play

DESCRIPTION   Three players hold hands and swing them in rhythm, counting to five. After they say five, they drop hands and place their right hands either palm facing down or palm facing up on their left hands. If two players place their hands the same way and the third player places his hands differently, the player who placed his hands differently becomes the leader. If all three players place their hands the same way, the game is repeated.

Figure 10

66   Oral games, rhymes and songs for beginners

in the early stages of learning (see Chapters 3 and 4). As simple games have the same basic beginning and ending and have to be sustained in the same sort of way, the same routines can be used for all games played in the first lessons. Also, since many games have more or less the same form (for example, card games involve giving out, counting and collecting cards; chasing games involve running to a safe 'home' area), the same routines can be used for all games of the same type. Thus, once the type of game has been learned, it is relatively easy and quick to teach a second game of the same type.

In the first lessons, the same few simple routines are sufficient for organising and managing games. These routines can be repeated more frequently than in playing the same game in Language 1. Once the routines have been established it is then possible to expand and introduce new ones (see Figure 11). With help from the teacher (for example, by asking questions to stimulate replies, like 'How many?' 'Is it your turn?'), children begin to develop interpersonal communication. As soon as some children know the routines, they can begin to organise the games, taking the role of the teacher. The teacher should then take the role of a player, interacting with the 'new teacher' and showing the children how to develop language (see the following checklists).

Checklist of language for starting a game

Stand here   Stand behind here
Stand behind this line
Make a circle
Sit down   Cross your legs
Follow me   Do like me
Give out the cards
Give one to everyone   Give two to everyone
Are you ready?

Let's start
Shut your eyes   Don't look
Count to five/ten
You're the first   You're the second
You're the last
You start
Look everyone

Checklist of language for sustaining a game

My turn   Your turn   It's your turn
Who's next?   He's next   She's next
Look! your card   It's your card
Take a card   Take two cards
They are your cards   Take them
Put them back   Put them back on the table
It's your turn again   Another turn
Again   Try again
Show him   Show him what to do

Checklist of language for ending a game

Stop   It's time to stop
Have you finished?
Count the cards   One card, two cards, etc
How many cards have you got?
You're the winner
Put the cards away   Put the things away

Figure 11 Introducing the game *how many?*

Frequency of game	Management/organising language			Game language	Teacher's role	Child's role
	Starting	Sustaining	Ending			
First time	Sit down Look (*pointing to cards*)	Yes No (*shaking head*)	Finished?	How many? one two three	All management and game language	(Listening) one two three
Second time	Sit down Are you ready? Look	Yes, good No	Finished? Count (*pointing to cards*) one two three etc	How many? one four two five three	All management and game language	(Listening) one four two five three
Third time	Sit down Are you ready? Look Yes Your turn, John	Yes, good No Your turn next Quickly	Stop. Finished? Count (*pointing to cards*) one two three four five etc	How many? one → ten	All management and game language	Yes one → ten Counting cards in response to teacher's question 'How many?'
Fourth time	As above No new language Concentrating on building up interaction				Teacher plays child's role	A child plays teacher's role Other children as above

5.3 Introducing and organising games

The first few times a game is played, the teacher organises and manages it totally. As children gain in oral fluency, they take it in turns to play the role of the teacher and direct the game. The teacher should then participate in the game as a player, but be ready to offer a word of advice or act as a referee where the occasion arises.

Children need to know exactly how to play a game; they need to know all the rules. When children are not sure what to do, chaos can result, particularly in chasing games, or there can be some confusion whereby a child thinks he has won, but in actual fact he has broken the rules inadvertently and been accused by the others of cheating. This can hurt a child so much that he refuses to play games for some time.

As children get used to playing a game, the speed of playing increases and it is more fun. Then it is possible to extend the length of play. However, it is important to stop play before children get tired as they lose interest; the ideal time to stop is when the children still want another turn.

Games need to be fun. Teachers will often find that, apart from sustaining interest in a game, they will also have to add some fun. This may be done by a well-timed hesitation, or by playing a card slowly, making a guess, changing the tone of voice to be mysterious or even by playing the wrong card on purpose to raise a laugh. Teachers may also find that where a game is a bit slow they have to speed it up by temporarily intervening. If games get a bit too noisy, teachers can encourage children to use loud whispers and if this does not work often the only solution is to move outside to the playground or change the game.

Some young children do not want to participate in games, especially in chasing games. It is better not to insist but to let them watch or help the teacher until they are at the correct stage of 'readiness' for particpation.

Discipline troubles generally arise when a child does not understand the game and cannot participate fully. In these cases it is a good idea for the teacher to play with the child for one or two turns. If this is impossible, a child who is good at the game can be asked to help.

In some games children have to drop out – for example, after being caught. There should be some special place in the classroom where children know they should stand and wait, watching the game until it is finished. Children appear to learn whilst watching. Most children like watching, but some become restless. These children can go back to their places and get on with colouring a picture, reading a book or finishing some work until the game is over. It is important that they have something definite to do otherwise discipline problems can arise.

If some children are not getting sufficient opportunity to use English even though they have a turn, teachers can stimulate use of English by asking children a few questions during the game, for example 'How many cards have you?' 'Is it your turn next?' Where classes are large, children can work in pairs or in small groups rather than as individuals. An alternative where classes are large is for one group to help the teacher whilst the other groups play. In most games described in this book a pair or group can be substituted for the individual.

The first time a game of a specific type, for example a card game, is introduced, teachers may find it necessary to explain it in Language 1. However, once one of a type of game has been played, it is usually no longer necessary to use Language 1, when introducing another game of the same type.

Many teachers find it better to introduce a game by starting to play it and explaining the rules during the game as the situation arises. At the end of the game the teacher can then explain that it was only a 'trial' and that now they are going to start playing properly. To explain all the rules of a game at the beginning without concrete examples is too confusing for young children.

5.4 Collecting, adapting and making games

Teachers will find it a good idea to keep their own book of suitable games. Many games are too advanced linguistically for young children but with some adaptation can be made suitable. The most effective games are often those made by a teacher or adapted to fit the needs and local conditions of the children she teaches. Some teachers are hesitant to make their own games because they think their standard of drawing is not high. This in itself is not important, and anyway, in most classes there are generally one or two children capable of illustrating games cards and keen to show off their skill.

Once children understand how to make cards and games boards, *Snakes and Ladders* and *Bingo*, for example, they should be encouraged to make their own examples of games which they can play with in the lesson. This can also be meaningful and satisfying as a way of practising handwriting.

TYPES OF GAMES
Oral games for young beginners can be divided into three groups:

1 Starting games. The type of game played before another game to find a leader or catcher or to decide who will play first.
2 Phase One quick games. Played in the first phase of the lesson. These games only last a few minutes and are played to consolidate a point or change the atmosphere.
3 Phase Three games. Longer games played in the third phase of a lesson. They can involve more movement, such as running or hiding, or consolidate a language point taught in Phases One and Two.

The games given in the next section have worked very well in practice for many teachers. For more ideas, a very large selection of games is available in *Which Game? – an ELT source book* by Betty Morgan Bowen which is itself a companion to another book by

Shelagh Rixon in this series: *How to use games in language teaching*.

5.5 Selection of games

It is important to realise that these games have been selected and in some cases adapted for very young beginners. The classification 'Any age' referring to suitable age should be taken to imply between four and nine years.

BIG OR LITTLE

Starting game

LEVEL Any level
AGE Any age
PLAYERS 2 players
TIMING 2 minutes
LOCATION Inside/Outside
MATERIALS A big
and little pencil

Aural/Oral
GAME LANGUAGE
Point to/Touch the big one
This is the big one
This is the little one

DESCRIPTION One player takes two pencils of different lengths and hides them so that one end of both pencils is hidden in the fist of his hand and the other end of the pencils sticks out the same amount. The player then asks the other player 'Point to the big one' or 'Touch the big one'. If that player guesses correctly, he wins and is the leader or first to play.
DEVELOPMENT The other player can be asked to identify 'the little one'

Figure 12(a)

LISTEN AND DO

LEVEL Beginners
AGE Young children
PLAYERS All class
TIMING 5 minutes
LOCATION Inside/Outside
MATERIALS None

Aural/Oral
GAME LANGUAGE
Stand up   Clap
Jump   Dance
Hop   Sit down

DESCRIPTION The teacher chooses a child and says, 'Stand up' and the child stands up. The leader continues giving commands until she says, 'Sit down', which ends the turn. If the player makes a mistake and does not carry out an instruction correctly he has to sit down straight away and the game begins with another player.

DEVELOPMENT As oral fluency develops, instructions can be extended to 'Jump three times', 'Hop twice', 'Clap four times'. Instructions can be further extended to 'Stand up quickly'. 'Run to the door'. 'Hop to the window'. 'Come here'. 'Sit down slowly'. When children learn to read, written instructions on flash cards can alternate with oral instructions or replace oral instructions.

Figure 12(b)

TOUCH YOUR NOSE

Quick game

LEVEL Beginners
AGE Young children
PLAYERS Individuals
         in group
TIMING 5 minutes
LOCATION Inside/Outside
MATERIALS None

Aural/Oral
GAME LANGUAGE
Touch your (+ part of face)
Don't touch (+ part of face)

DESCRIPTION The teacher says 'Touch your nose' and all the players touch their nose with one hand or finger. The teacher then says 'Touch your eye,' and the children touch their eye. The game continues until the teacher says, 'Don't touch your ear.' Any player who moves their hand in the direction of their ear or touches their ear is out of the game. The game continues until all or nearly all the players are out. The game then starts again.

DEVELOPMENT To include parts of the body. To add 'Touch your right ear,' or 'Don't touch your left leg.'

Figure 12(c)

HOW MANY?

LEVEL Beginners
AGE Young children
PLAYERS Individuals
      in group
TIMING 5 minutes
LOCATION Inside/Outside
MATERIALS Cards with
      Arabic numbers
      and words

Aural/Oral
Recognition of Arabic
numerals or words
GAME LANGUAGE
How many?
One to Ten

DESCRIPTION 15 cards with numbers 1, 2 or 3 on
one side are placed number side down on a table,
mat or floor. The teacher points to one card and says
'How many?' looking at a child. Child replies one, two
or three. Teacher turns over the card. If the child
has guessed correctly, teacher gives the card to the
child. If the child guesses incorrectly, the teacher
replaces the card. The teacher then asks
another child. The child with the most cards wins.
DEVELOPMENT Cards with numbers 4 and 5 are
added, then further cards with numbers up to 10.
Cards with written numbers can be introduced
gradually to replace Arabic numbers.
REMARK This type of game can be played with
cards of pictures of thing and word for example
picture of a book and word card 'a book'.
The question asked is 'What's this?'
The same game can be played with
colours with question 'What's this?'

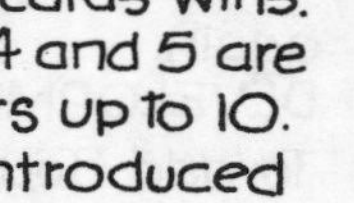

Figure 12(d)

WHERE'S THE MONKEY?

LEVEL Beginners
AGE Young children
PLAYERS All class
TIMING 5-10 minutes
LOCATION Outside/Inside
MATERIALS A soft toy
Children like to
take it in turns
to bring one of
their soft toys
to hide

Aural/Oral
GAME LANGUAGE
Where's the monkey?
Here's the monkey
Here it is

DESCRIPTION Players shut their eyes and count
to ten, whilst the teacher hides the toy monkey, or
some other soft toy, anywhere in the room or
garden. The players then open their eyes and the
teacher says, 'Where's the monkey?' The players
repeat, 'Where's the monkey?' and run to look for
the monkey. The player who finds the monkey holds
it up and says, 'Here's the monkey'.
The game begins again with the finder hiding
the monkey.
DEVELOPMENT Teacher can ask the children
'Is the monkey on the chair?' 'Is the monkey near
the door?' etc. Two toys can be hidden and
teacher asks, 'Where are the ....
and the ....?' The finder replies
'Here they are'.

Figure 12(e)

WHAT ARE YOU DOING NOW?

LEVEL Beginners
AGE Young children
PLAYERS All class
TIMING 5-10 minutes
LOCATION Outside/Inside
           (space required)
MATERIALS None

Aural/Oral
GAME LANGUAGE
What's he doing?
What's he doing now?
He's dancing/singing etc
Yes, I am/No, I'm not

DESCRIPTION One player stands in the middle of a circle. The teacher whispers to the player an instruction for example, 'Laugh'. The other players walk round the circle saying,

What's he doing?
What's he doing?
What's he doing now?

whilst the player in the middle mimes the instruction. The player continues whilst the teacher asks someone to guess what he is doing. If the guess is correct, the players exchange places. If the guess is incorrect, the game starts again with the players unchanged.

DEVELOPMENT The teacher gives more complex instructions, for example, 'Eat an ice cream'.

Figure 12(f)

WHAT'S THE TIME MR WOLF?

LEVEL Beginners	Aural/Oral
AGE Young children	GAME LANGUAGE
PLAYERS All class	What's the time, Mr Wolf?
TIMING 5-10 minutes	One o'clock
LOCATION Outside/Inside	Two o'clock etc
(space required)	Dinner time
MATERIALS None	

DESCRIPTION Mr Wolf stands in his 'house' at
one end of the room. The players, the sheep,
stand in their 'house' behind a line, at the other
end of the room. The sheep ask Mr Wolf, 'What's
the time, Mr Wolf?' and Mr Wolf replies, 'One o'clock'.
The sheep walk a little closer to Mr Wolf and again
ask the question. Mr Wolf replies, 'Two o'clock.'
They again walk a little closer and ask. Mr Wolf
replies, 'Three o'clock' The game continues until
Mr Wolf replies, 'Dinner time', and chases the sheep
back to their 'house'. If he catches any before
they reach their house, they stay at Mr Wolf's
house for a turn. The teacher changes Mr Wolf
as she wishes.

DEVELOPMENT 'Half past' and other meal times
like 'breakfast time',
'tea time' can be
introduced, but
Mr Wolf still chases
on 'dinner time'.

Figure 12(g)

5.6 Rhymes and songs

Children learn rhymes easily and quickly and they appear to enjoy learning them and reciting them. Rhymes are prefabricated language. Most are made up of prefabricated phrases; and ones where new words are slotted into the same verse or a different verse, are similar to prefabricated routines (see Chapter 1).

Young beginners seem to feel that when they can say a rhyme, they can speak a lot of English quickly rather like an adult and this is something that they appear to want to do. Rhymes are a bonus in language learning. Although they should be integrated within a lesson plan, they can be learned in addition to other language items. Rhymes introduce children naturally and effectively to the complete sounds of English as well as to stress and intonation. They are also a way of giving children a complete text with a complete piece of meaning from the very first lesson. Isolated items of language, especially if not linked to situations, are often much more difficult for young beginners to understand, use or remember. If rhymes are specially selected, they can be used to introduce new language or to consolidate. The example in Figure 13 can be used in both these ways (Dunn 1979: 10).

This illustration is planned to be an educational aid. The children can count the apples and the figures in it. When the children know the rhyme, it can be used:

  a for teaching other plurals, eg one cat, two cats.
  b as a game. Any child who adds the name of an object after saying *four*, drops out of the game.

Language learned in a rhyme can often be transferred to other situations in the classroom.

> Goodbye everyone,
> Goodbye everyone,
> Goodbye everyone,
> It's time to say goodbye.

One apple,
Two apples,
Three apples,
Four.
Five apples,
Six apples,
Seven apples,
Any more?

Figure 13

In the above rhyme the word 'everyone' can be transferred to add on to prefabricated phrases like 'Sit down' which have already been learned. 'It's time to . . .' can be transferred to other situations like, 'It's time to go home.' 'It's time to have a snack.' 'It's time to play a game.'

Some traditional rhymes (for example, 'Solomon Grundy') are part of English culture, but include difficult language, which may be impossible to transfer in the classroom. They are better left until Part Two.

RHYME TIME

It is useful to begin every lesson (see Figure 8) with a special Rhyme Time when children gather round the teacher. If Rhyme Time takes the same form in each lesson, the children know what to expect. Rhyme Time can begin by running through familiar rhymes, rhyme-games and songs. After this 'warming-up' period children are ready to move on to new and unfamiliar material. In these initial few minutes a selection of rhymes familiar to the children is chosen and each rhyme is repeated twice by the teacher and children together. If the teacher feels it is necessary, she can repeat one or more of the rhymes again herself, perhaps altering the tone of her voice, which adds an element of excitement. After this the teacher can select groups of children to say the rhyme in turn, for example, boys, girls, all girls wearing red. In this way the rhyme is repeated several more times, and changing the groups so that the children are sometimes standing, sometimes sitting and the waiting for 'your turn' gives an added suspense and injects the fun typical of many games. As children repeat rhymes over and over again, they are continually refining their pronunciation and increasing their oral fluency.

When introducing a new rhyme, the teacher should repeat it first, clearly and slowly, being careful not to distort the speech patterns by, for example, using strong forms instead of weak forms for *the* and *a*. Illustrations can be used to explain the meaning of the rhyme and, if advisable and possible, teachers can give a rough translation once in the children's mother tongue. The rhyme should be repeated a second time by the teacher, who can then select groups of children to say it again with her. At this stage of learning children should not be expected to repeat rhymes without the lead being given by the model speaker. As children get more practice in learning rhymes, they appear to be able to learn new ones more quickly.

Many teachers have found that except for very gifted children, who learn complete rhymes straight away, most children learn only certain words of a new rhyme in the first lesson. These are generally information words. Different classes of beginners have been able to remember all of the following rhyme except the underlined words by the end of the first lesson.

One, two, three,
Clap with me
Clap, clap, clap
Clap like me.

In the next lesson, after repeating the rhyme once together with the teacher or model speaker, most children were able to say the complete rhyme by themselves.

Learning is undoubtedly helped if the new rhyme is repeated again once or twice, in chorus with the children, when they come together at the end of the lesson just before saying goodbye.

RECORDINGS
Teachers who are uncertain of their own pronunciation when saying rhymes can use a cassette recorder and pre-recorded cassettes instead of their own voice. However, results are better if the teacher herself first works with the recording to improve her own English, and then teaches the children the rhymes herself, as the personal relationship is very important in learning. Once the children have learned the rhyme with the teacher, they can listen

to the recording and refine their own pronunciation from the recorded model (see the section on pronunciation in Chapter 4).

Families who possess cassette or record players can help their children consolidate by setting aside some time after the children have come home from school for listening to the recording. This could be done every night or once or twice a week. It is also useful if the teacher sends the children home with a short note, in print handwriting (see Dunn 1984: Chapter 2), telling the parent what rhyme or rhymes to listen to.

Figure 14

RHYME BOOKS

Even if children cannot yet read, they enjoy having their own copy of a book of rhymes. The illustrations are often sufficient to stimulate them to repeat the rhyme to themselves silently or aloud. Apart from the enjoyment and the importance of developing a love of books, this helps to consolidate language learning.

Many children teach themselves to read through rhymes. This is done with the help of flash cards. First they are introduced to flash cards of words in three or four rhymes they know well. Then they put the flash cards in sequence to 'write' the rhymes. Finally they are ready to read the rhymes in the book. Once they have had the experience of being able to read some rhymes in the rhyme book, many then go on to teach themselves to read other rhymes from the book that they already know orally. The advantage of learning to read through rhymes is that since children know the text so well orally, they quickly pass from reading word by word to reading complete phrases, using correct intonation, stress and pronunciation (see Chapter 4).

SONGS

A few songs or singing games can be included in Rhyme Time; but, as in the choice of rhymes, songs and singing games should be selected for their suitable language content (see Figure 15). Traditional songs with difficult language and vocabulary or complicated music are best left to Part Two. Songs which distort special patterns or pronunciation are best avoided at this early stage of learning. It should be remembered that it is more difficult for children to transfer language from songs than from rhymes as they have first to put the language into spoken form. To help children over this difficulty, it is a good idea to sometimes 'say' songs instead of singing them.

Some teachers set their own words to well-known songs, which makes learning the words easier as the children already know the music.

Figure 15

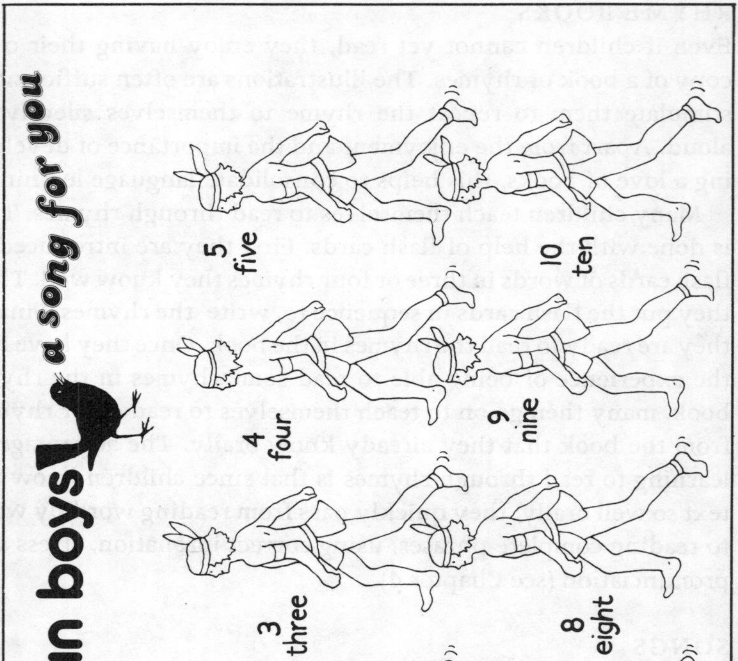

Ten little Indian boys
a song for you

Colour the ten little Indian boys.

1 one	2 two	3 three	4 four	5 five
6 six	7 seven	8 eight	9 nine	10 ten

Teachers wishing to explore further the possibilities of the activities mentioned in this Chapter should consult *Developing English with young learners* (Dunn 1984). The first chapter of this companion book considers how rhymes, songs and games can be used to introduce informally the letters of the alphabet. Teachers are given suggestions for how they can build on any knowledge children already have (often gained from these activities) to develop the skills of reading and writing.

References

Asian Cultural Centre for UNESCO, *Let's Play Asian Children's Games*, (1978 – reprinted 1980 in association with Macmillan Southeast Asia (Pte) Ltd).

Corder S Pit, 'Error Analysis, Interlanguage and Second Language Learning', *Language Teaching and Linguistics: Surveys*, (Cambridge: Cambridge University Press, 1977).

Donaldson M, *Children's Minds*, (London: Fontana, 1978).

Donoghue M R and Kunkle J F, *Second Language in Primary Education*, (London: Newbury House, 1979).

Dunn O, *Mr Bear's Book of Rhymes*, (London: Macmillan, 1979) (cassette).

Dunn O, *The Gingerbread Boy*, Ranger Story Workbooks, (London: Macmillan, 1979).

Dunn O, *Developing English with young learners*, (London: Macmillan, 1984).

Elliot A J, *Child Language*, (Cambridge: Cambridge University Press, 1981).

Garvie C, *Play*, (London: Fontana, 1979).

Goodacre E J, *Methods of Reading*, (London: Centre for the teaching of reading, Reading University).

Hawkes N, *Communication in the classroom*, edited by Johnson K and Morrow K, (London: Longman, 1981).

Krashen S D, *Second Language Acquisition and Second Language Learning*, (Oxford: Pergamon Institute of English, 1981).

Morgan Bowen B, *Look Here! Visual Aids in Language Teaching*, (London: Macmillan, 1982).

Bowen B Morgan, *Which Game? – an ELT source book*, (London: Macmillan, forthcoming).

Norrish J, *Language learners and their errors*, (London: Macmillan, 1983).

The Plowden Report, *Children in their Primary Schools*, (HMSO: 1967).

Pluckrose H, *Children in their Primary Schools*, (London: Penguin, 1979).

Rixon S, *How to use games in language teaching*, (London: Macmillan, 1981).

Schools Council, *Scope; an introductory course for immigrant children*, Stage 1, Teacher's Book (1969).

Swain M, 'Time and Timing in Bilingual Education', *Journal of Applied Linguistics*, Volume 31, (1981).

Tench P, *Pronunciation skills*, (London: Macmillan, 1981).

Tucker N, *What is a child?* (London: Fontana, 1977).

de Villiers PA and de Villiers JG, *Early Language*, (London: Fontana, 1979).

Ward S Aristotelous, *Dippitydoo: Songs and Activities for Children*, (London: Longman, 1981).

Wells G, *Language through action – the study of language development,* (London: Cambridge University Press, 1981).